How Two Minds Meet

Also by *Beth Baumert*

When Two Spines Align: Dressage Dynamics

(PRINT AND EPUB)

Beth Baumert

How Two Minds Meet

The Mental Dynamics of Dressage

Trafalgar Square
North Pomfret, Vermont

First published in 2020 by
Trafalgar Square Books
North Pomfret, Vermont 05053

Disclaimer of Liability
The author and publisher shall have neither liability nor responsibility to any person or entity with respect to any loss or damage caused or alleged to be caused directly or indirectly by the information contained in this book. While the book is as accurate as the author can make it, there may be errors, omissions, and inaccuracies.

Trafalgar Square Books encourages the use of approved safety helmets in all equestrian sports and activities.

Library of Congress Cataloging-in-Publication Data

Names: Baumert, Beth, author.
Title: How two minds meet : the mental dynamics of dressage / Beth Baumert.

Description: North Pomfret : Trafalgar Square Books, 2020. | Includes
    index. | Summary: "In dressage trainer Beth Baumert's new book she takes
    us beyond physical harmony to look at the minds of both horse and rider,
    each complete with its own set of emotions and mental capabilities. Not
    only does Baumert explain how to optimize the use of the "thinking mind"
    in order to become a better learner in the saddle, she provides
    techniques for maximizing mental and emotional harmony with the horse, a
    state of unity that feels so good, Baumert calls it the "charming
    addiction"-once a rider has it, she wants to attain it again and again.
    Feeding this addiction is possible, says Baumert, with the thoughtful,
    practical insight she shares in these pages"-- Provided by publisher.
Identifiers: LCCN 2020030491 (print) | LCCN 2020030492 (ebook) | ISBN
    9781570769726 (Paperback) | ISBN 9781646010790 (ePub)
Subjects: LCSH: Dressage--Psychological aspects. | Dressage
    horses--Training. | Dressage--Handbooks, manuals, etc.
Classification: LCC SF309.5 .B384 2020 (print) | LCC SF309.5 (ebook) |
    DDC 798.2/3--dc23
LC record available at https://lccn.loc.gov/2020030491
LC ebook record available at https://lccn.loc.gov/2020030492

Illustrations by Sandy Rabinowitz.
Diagrams by Lauryl Eddlemon except p. 198, which is reprinted with permission from the USDF (usdf.org).

Photo credits: Beth Baumert (pp. 30, 56, 61, 69); Kevin Baumert (p. 112); Arnd Bronkhorst/arnd.nl (pp. viii, 16, 23, 35, 39, 40, 46, 93, 115, 148, 160, 166, 194); Frank Sorge/arnd.nl (pp. 19, 22); Amy Dragoo/arnd.nl (pp. 8, 24); Jacques Toffi (pp. 25, 26); Paula da Silva/arnd.nl (pp. 39, 106); Shannon Brinkman/arnd.nl (p. 122); Pierre Costabadie/arnd.nl (p. 133); Charles Mann/arnd.nl (p. 172); den-belitsky/stock.adobe.com (p. 64); FotoLL/stock.adobe.com (pp. 74, 75); EtiAmmos/stock.adobe.com (p. 76); dragonstock/stock.adobe.com (p. 88); by-studio/stock.adobe.com (p. 98); Monet/stock.adobe.com (p. 118); Cristina Conti/stock.adobe.com (p. 128); escapejaja/stock.adobe.com (pp. 140, 141); Choat/stock.adobe.com (p. 142)

Book design by *Katarzyna Misiukanis–Celińska*
Cover design by *RM Didier*
Index by *Andrea Jones (JonesLiteraryServices.com)*
Typefaces: *Minion Pro, Myriad Pro* and *Roboto*

Printed in China

10 9 8 7 6 5 4 3 2 1

Contents

Contents

Contents

INTRODUCTION

How Two Minds Meet:
The Mental Dynamics
of Dressage

● **{I.1}** If you imagine that you're wearing Charlotte DuJardin's gloves, your connection might somehow improve, and your horse might become even more expressive. How does that happen?

The *Possibility* of Magic

If you tell a rider to put her brain in her butt, she'll sit better. If you tell her to lighten her heart, she'll feel better. If you tell a jumper rider to pretend she's in Beezie Madden's boots, she and her horse will both jump better. If you tell a dressage rider to pretend she's wearing the gloves of British dressage star Charlotte Dujardin, she'll have a better connection and her horse will move better. What's up with that? When a rider sits on a horse with an extraordinary half-pass, she will be able to develop her next horse so as to achieve the same half-pass. How does this happen?

The fact of the matter is that there's a mind-body connection within the rider that is rarely tapped, and there's a mind-body connection within the horse, and between the horse and rider, that can and should be explored further. And there's that whisper of a mental connection between horse and rider that should be maximized.

Human minds are typically used for analytical, logical thinking. We figure things out and we learn; that's what we do. That "thinking" mind is where you learned the basics of what Charlotte Dujardin was doing in the first place, but when you *saw* her and you *saw* her horse, Valegro, either in person or on video, a different part of your mind kicked in (fig. I.1). Then when you, as a rider, pulled on Charlotte's imaginary gloves, there wasn't much logic happening. You were tapping an altogether different dimension of the mind.

Of course, there is a mind-body connection within the horse, too. He learns about the basics, and then as he truly understands—in his head—how movements feel, he becomes somewhat cultured about more and more aspects of the physical work. He lacks the analytical thinking powers of his rider, so he does not aspire to be as good as another horse, and he has no goals for improvement, but he does know what a movement *feels* like. He knows that jumping a fence with good balance feels good and is fun. He knows that doing a leg-yield by using his body with integrity feels good, and he knows that you praise him when it feels good, so he needs less and less encouragement to perform well.

In fact, as the horse understands and has the desire to reproduce the nice feeling in his body—even when it requires great effort—the rider only needs very tiny aids to ask for whatever she wants. Then, it seems (can it be true?), that all you need to do is think of what you want, and your horse does it. How can that be? Did you give an aid, or did you really only *think* canter? Did you have a mental picture of canter, and then your horse saw it? Was it a matter of extrasensory perception (ESP)?

Was your horse perceiving your wishes without any physical cue at all? Does that really happen? Most would say yes.

● The Physical, Emotional, and Mental

My previous book, *When Two Spines Align: Dressage Dynamics,* is all about how the physical bodies of horse and rider work together. The book explains the physical technique and the science—the physics—behind riding in balance. When the horse is in physical balance, he's comfortable and using his body in a way

Without considering the mind and the heart, riding would become sadly mechanical and without beauty.

that will build strength and suppleness rather than breaking it down from tension. That book is about technique, but without considering the mind and the heart, riding would become sadly mechanical and without beauty. We'd miss the point, because horses are all about spirit. They challenge us to involve our hearts and minds.

In this book, I'll go beyond the physical harmony attained in *When Two Spines Align* and look at the horse's mind, complete with emotions and mental capabilities, and the rider's mind with its own set of emotions and mental capabilities. You'll look at how to maximize the use of your thinking mind so you can be a better learner, and then you'll look into those other dimensions of the mind to learn how to maximize harmony, not only physically, but also mentally and emotionally.

This state of harmony between horse and rider feels like magic, and once you get a hint of what the unity feels like, you will want it again and again. It can, in fact, become a bit of an obsession. I call it the "charming addiction, " because we are so charmed by the horse-and-rider potential that we often get overly absorbed in the pursuit of that perfection. It's kind of a positive addiction.

Why do many of us have this addiction to horses? Maybe it's because horses require that we use more than the thinking mind. They give you access to—and actually require that you explore—other dimensions of the mind. These other dimensions of the mind require that you find your higher self. Maybe that's why so many of us have succumbed to the "charming addiction."

In the process, after technique is mastered, horse and rider cross the threshold and enter the world of art where the two become one, and the true beauty and spirit of the horse emerge. That further feeds the addiction.

In Part One of this book, I examine how the mind of the horse works. In Part Two, I look at the rider's two minds—the analytical mind and the non-thinking or sensory dimension of the mind that the horse more readily identifies with. In Part Three, I talk about the Nine Principles of Learning that enable you to maximize learning in the traditional, knowledge-accumulating part of your brain. Here's a more detailed peek at what I cover in each part:

● Part One—*The Horse's Amazing Mind*

How does the horse's mind work? Some people mistakenly feel that horses aren't very intelligent, but they are simply different from us—intelligent in a different way. First, horses are positive by nature, so negative messages don't work. Horses understand positive messages perfectly well. Second, horses live rather completely in the present, so they are not analytical thinkers. You can't present the horse with complex problems and be successful. Horses have little consideration for the past and the future. They primarily experience the

3

"now." And that's the place where you need to go to meet them. In the "now," the horse learns by repetition, reward, association, clarity, and persistent consistency. In this way, they are remarkable learners.

The horse's emotions, however, sometimes get in the way. Horses easily revert to their innate "fight or flight" reflexes. As herd animals, in the face of fear they want to turn to a leader for confidence and guidance. If you're the rider, you need to be the leader, and you want to be a trusted leader so he learns that he can turn to you in lieu of fight or flight. You, as the rider, want to teach your horse without triggering his innate fight or flight reflexes. You want your horse to be emotionally trusting, physically comfortable and mentally engaged.

● Part Two—*The Rider's Multiple Minds*

How can you, as a rider, best use your mind to work with your horse? The best riders ride with two minds: one that the horse *cannot* read and one that he *can* read. Your horse doesn't have access to your analytical, thinking mind, but you can meet him in the non-thinking, sensory place where you're imagining how, for example, a better trot feels. He can "hear" you and understands you when you're coming from the right frame of mind.

Riders often complain, "My horse isn't listening to me! " But clear communication is a two-way street and must consistently come from the right place. I'll explore ways to get into that non-thinking place where the best communication takes place.

Just as emotions sometimes plague horses, they're a factor with riders too. Emotion is the

Once you get a hint of what the unity feels like, you will want it again and again.

underlying attitude with which we couch the things we think and do. Emotion is either the delicious sauce that enhances our thoughts and actions, or it minimizes our chances of success by poisoning our thoughts and actions. Communication with horses requires that we meet them on their level of thinking—or non-thinking—and we'll explore how our horses require that we be our best selves by being positive, compassionate, and "present."

● Part Three—*The Nine Principles of Learning*

Principles of Learning have been developed by educational psychologists as ways to maximize the learning abilities of teachers and students. By utilizing these Principles, instructors can improve their teaching abilities, and riders can improve their learning abilities—and the learning abilities of their horses.

Part Three of this book is dedicated to a discussion of the Nine Principles and their specific ways of maximizing your ability to learn, retain, and apply knowledge that's useful when training horses. The ninth and final principle of learning involves the organization of your knowledge. Information is best utilized when knowledge is categorized. How efficient is your brain's filing system? In the Appendix (see p. 196), you can look at two specific categories of knowledge that will help you.

● The Possibilities Are Endless

As I was writing *When Two Spines Align: Dressage Dynamics,* I knew that I would finish it. The writing would end because the physics of balancing horse and rider is finite. Exploring the mind is different because the possibilities are endless. This book is only a smattering of thoughts that I hope will serve as a launching point for your own individual journey. I'd like this book to open up new ways for you to enjoy your horse and improve your riding and training.

Throughout these pages, you'll see that I digress from the subject of "Two Minds" (the mental) back to "Two Spines" (the physical). It can't be helped because a certain amount of technique is necessary. When your horse isn't physically comfortable, there can't be any meeting of the minds, and the best way to make your horse comfortable, aside from the practice of good horsemanship, is to balance your horse under saddle. When he's out of balance, there's a certain amount of physical and mental tension and discomfort. Colored sidebars throughout contain information on the techniques of balancing your horse physically. That's the best place to start when your goal is a meeting of the minds.

NOTE: *The rider, in these pages, is always referred to as "she" and the horse as "he." This is only for convenience. No disrespect is intended toward men and mares. I'm very fond of both. In addition, the rider is often referred to as a "trainer" because every rider is a trainer in the sense that whenever she sits on a horse, the horse will be better or worse tomorrow as a result of today's ride.*

PART ONE

The Horse's Amazing Mind

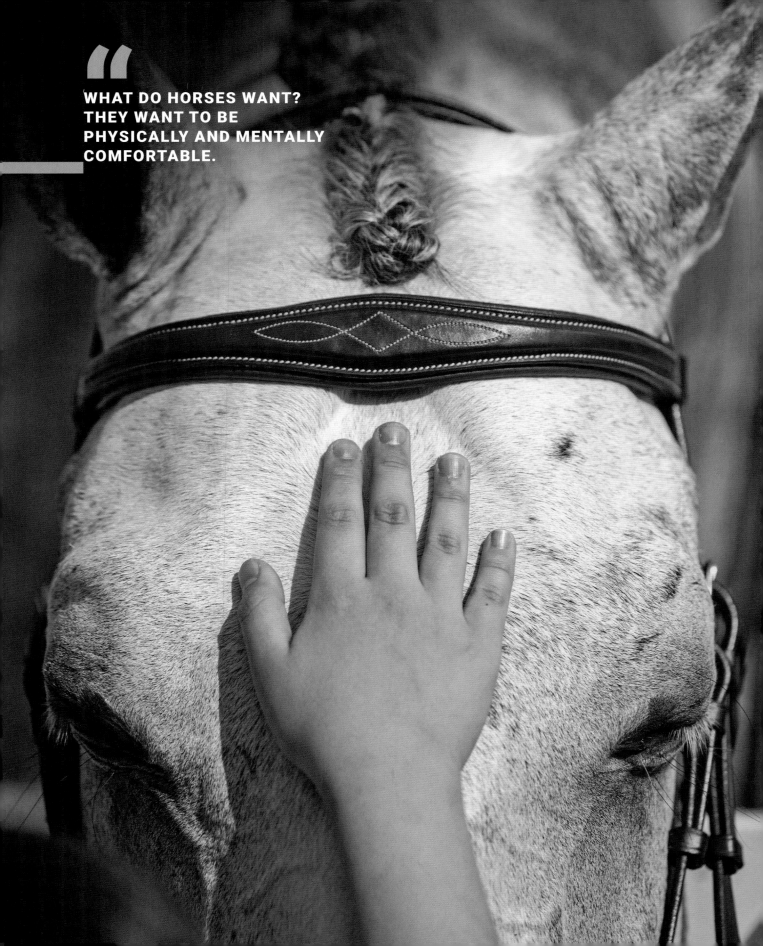

The Horse's State of Mind

1

Humans are thinkers (fig. 1.1). That is what we do best, but in the presence of horses, we are transported to a very special non-thinking place. That's the allure. It's the cause of our addiction. Horses bring us to their state of mind where there is no wrangling with daily problems; they don't even consider long-term issues or lofty goals. They don't understand negativity and they live primarily in the present moment. They have limited ability to be sorry for yesterday's misstep—or pumped up about yesterday's victory. They don't feel sorry that you hurt your shoulder when you fell off, and they don't connive to get rid of you tomorrow. They can have pure self-esteem unassociated with yesterday's Olympic gold-medal victory or Kentucky Derby win.

Horses are incapable of introspection, so they can't have self-pity and they can't pass judgment. Wow. What a world. Let's look specifically at some of the gifts horses bring to us because of how they use their minds.

● Horses Live in the Present

It's been said that "the present" is a gift, and from the horse, it is an extraordinary one. Horses primarily experience *now*, so to communicate with them successfully, you need to be in the *now* also. Their *now* isn't completely pure, however, because horses carry a lasting impression of the past with them. Their experience from past *nows* brings them to today with good or bad "baggage." The horse doesn't brood over the past, but that baggage is simply a factual backdrop for this moment's experiences.

Horses bring us to their state of mind where there is no wrangling with daily problems.

In contrast, let's talk for a moment about humans. They do think about the baggage, and they live in the world of the clock for the most part. We're taught, from an early age, to learn from our past mistakes and plan for the future. So, for example, we're sorry that we didn't study for the eighth grade history exam, and we plan to set aside more time for studying history next semester.

When we are "with" our horses mentally and physically, they set us free from both the past and the future. There is no guilt or remorse about yesterday's failure, nor is there delight or gloating over yesterday's success; there are no worries about tomorrow's exciting or challenging plans. There is no thought of tomorrow. You and I can plan for tomorrow, the next day, and even next year if we have enough foresight, but that isn't shared with the horse. The horse cannot read the mind that is saying, "I hope that…," or "I wish that….," or "I'm planning to…." Those forward-thinking variable ambitions don't exist for the horse—he doesn't contemplate the future.

This moment—right now—is the only thing shared with the horse…and then the next moment…and the next. On a bounding horse, the *now* is a moving target! Horses are in the world of what "is," so they require their rider to be "present." Whereas we often think of the meditative state as being passive, when communicating from the saddle, it is a dynamic meditative state.

Awareness of the past and future do influence and inform the *now*. That is, the horse doesn't know about the schooling show or the Olympic Games next month, but what you do today—right

● {1.1} Humans are thinkers. We're taught to solve problems, and accolades fall to the one who outthinks everyone else. When with horses, however, we are transported to a very peaceful, non-thinking place.

11

now—is based on your plan for next month, and what you do right now does influence, positively or negatively, what will happen at the schooling show or the Olympic Games. Whereas horses don't mentally gather their successes, they also have no ability to gather their memories of failure. They have no self-pity and their self-esteem isn't based on the awards they've won (fig. 1.2).

The problem occurs when you think about the past or the future while you're riding your

*Horses primarily experience **now**, so to communicate with them successfully, you need to be in the **now** also.*

horse. He experiences that as abandonment or confusion—a feeling of having no leader. He needs your constant attention and concentration on what is happening in the moment. Riding is all about mental concentration. Once you learn that, you can use the past and the future with wisdom to constructively inform the present, and then you can truly concentrate on what you're doing.

What if we lived our entire lives this way? Well, we can—by concentrating on the present task at hand. We would become aware that the *now*— this very moment—is the only thing we can ever actually influence anyway. But we, fortunately, have the ability to switch between the present and the practical applications of experiences in the past, along with plans for the future. We have the ability to culture forward-thinking, variable ambitions as we devote ourselves totally to the present. The rider can think that she needs to achieve more bend in the shoulder-in without abandoning the horse mentally. She can switch between two methods of using her mind. We'll spend much more time, discussing those two minds in Part Two (see p. 75).

● {1.2} Horses don't have the mental ability to reflect on past successes or failures. As a result, they have no self-awareness, and their self-esteem isn't based on their past accomplishments.

How Two Minds Meet: The Mental Dynamics of Dressage

● Horses Experience Life in a Positive Way

Horses don't understand negatives. They do not understand *I hope she doesn't…, I wish she wouldn't…, Don't do this…, I'm afraid that….* They don't understand mental or emotional garbage, for example, I hope he doesn't refuse the fence, because I want to get out of this alive and I'm afraid I'll fall off like I did last week. This is a message that is negative, emotional, and convoluted. It's usually accompanied by a dreadful mental image that the horse has no trouble reading, and we all know how that story ends.

Since the horse doesn't understand the negative aspect of the message, he gets a message that goes like this: *Refuse the fence as I have in the past. Do it eagerly. My rider may end up on the ground.* Even the boldest, most willing jumper would, at least, become distracted or confused by his rider's message.

Boosting the Positive Possibility

The horses in training at a well-known stable were generally ridden by competent and kind professionals. They were also ridden by their owners and occasionally by other riders. Being ridden by more than one rider is rarely a problem, but the trainer at this facility learned that one skittish horse she had in training was getting very mixed messages.

Through her sound system, the trainer frequently heard the professional rider talking to the horse, "You're so brave. What a good boy." Or, "Come on, you can do it! Oh good."

Not surprisingly, the horse was often confident for this rider because that which you imagine often does become reality. The horse was getting constant encouraging messages about what he could and should do. She was steering him to correct choices.

One day, a different rider got on the same horse. Predictably, the horse spooked, and the trainer heard through her sound system, "Don't be a jerk! Cut it out! " The trainer suddenly understood the lack of consistent feedback this horse was getting. The horse was not only getting a negative message from his rider (which he didn't understand), but he wasn't being told what he *should* do. The rider wasn't being a leader—she was just being a disciplinarian. The use of that sound system helped the trainer realize the problem and enabled her to explain to the second rider how she might help the horse gain confidence. As an aside, to give the second rider some credit, she was nervous and would have been better off on a horse with a different temperament. ●

13

The rider must think positively.

German trainer Conrad Schumacher often told his dressage students, "You must have the WILL." He was usually referring to a line of tempi changes, and he often asked his rider to verbally call out "I WILL" when riding each change. The rider must know what she wants and have a very clear plan for achieving it. Horses train people to think clearly and positively.

For example, to jump a vertical fence or to ride a lengthened stride on the diagonal, the rider might go through these steps:

- Half-halt before the turn and balance through it.
- Half-halt again after the turn to straighten.
- Establish the length of stride you want and ride the line.
- Half-halt to rebalance after the lengthening or the fence.
- Reward! (Great job!)
- Rebalance and repeat....

Horses understand these positive, clear messages.

● Horses Don't Pass Judgment

Horses aren't critics. They don't look down upon a rider's lack of skill in the saddle. It is what it is. If a better rider gets on the horse, he will go better because of the superior skills, but he doesn't then begrudge the first rider. When the stable management is superior, the horse will flourish, but he doesn't look back on and resent a previous situation that wasn't so favorable. If the hay is outstanding, he doesn't compare it to what he had before and say, *What a relief.* He is simply

Although horses don't ponder the skill or lack of skill of the rider, they are left with that kernel of an impression that will give them confidence or anxiety the next time.

happy with the outstanding hay. In time, he will come to expect it and might reject poor hay, but he isn't introspective about it.

Whereas horses may have high or low self-esteem, they don't achieve it by pondering their achievements or their mistakes. They have high or low self-esteem first, by nature and second, from their trainer. They are incapable of introspection, because introspection would require they not be in the present. Lacking the capacity for introspection, they simply have a self-image they don't ponder or think about or try to improve. It just is.

They don't ponder yesterday's mishap—or joy—on the trail, but they will be left with a kernel of impression that may make them joyous or fearful on today's journey. Although horses don't ponder the skill or lack of skill of the rider, they are left with that kernel of an impression that will give them confidence or anxiety the next time. Over time, that kernel grows to become a solid impression of trust or distrust in a rider.

What do horses want? They want to be physically and mentally comfortable. In Part Two, I discuss the Comfort, Stretch, and Panic zones (see p. 71). Although learning doesn't happen in the Comfort Zone, it's an important place for horses and riders to spend relaxation time and gain confidence. Progress happens in the Stretch Zone where horses love being challenged within reason, gaining strength and competence. It's the same with human athletes.

Trainers teach by playing on the edges of these zones. They dabble in the Stretch Zone and return to the Comfort Zone. They know where their particular horse's Panic Zone is, and they don't play near it.

Good trainers never force their horses to perform. They help them make good choices. When the horse's body is in the ideal position, the desired outcome is the easiest choice for the horse. It's the most comfortable choice.

s u m m a r y   o f   c h a p t e r   1

Essential Information About Your Horse's State of Mind

✓ **Horses don't think about the past and the future.** They primarily experience the present moment—the *now*. To communicate with them successfully, you need to be transported to that place where you are attentive to the current moment.

✓ **Horses don't understand negativity.** They don't understand your thinking, *Don't spook at the terrifying tent*. In training, you need to tell them what you *want*—not what you *don't* want.

✓ **Horses don't pass judgment.** They don't mentally scold a rider for her clumsy aids. They will simply go better for a more skilled rider.

✓ **Horses want to be comfortable.** Although trainers challenge horses with discretion, the best trainers are very aware of the horse's comfort.

SUMMARY 1

"
ALL SUCCESSFUL HORSE-AND-RIDER
PARTNERSHIPS ARE BASED
ON UNDERSTANDING THE
HERD MENTALITY.

Leadership and Freedom— Meeting Your Horse's Herd Needs

Horses are herd animals, and when it comes to riding horses, the importance of this fact is often overlooked and underestimated (fig. 2.1). All successful horse-and-rider partnerships are based on understanding the herd mentality.

Members of the herd are free, but the cost of that freedom is that they must be on the lookout for danger (fig. 2.2).

As you know, by instinct, horses are "fight-or-flight" creatures, so they need a responsible leader to protect them in the face of threats. That's how horses are in the wild, and those inclinations are still with horses that have been domesticated. They still need a leader and they will either fight or run away in the face of danger. Although your horse may come to trust you as his leader, it will serve you well to keep his innate needs in mind.

The fear that provokes the fight-or-flight instinct in horses can be real or imagined. Under saddle, horses can fight by displaying a rolodex of common resistances such as bucking, rearing, chomping or grinding at the bit, tail-swishing, spooking, and so on, or they might flee—simply bolt and run away.

Real physical pain or discomfort can manifest itself in fear, too. We've all seen the horse that runs away from his own painful hocks or bucks from an uncomfortable saddle (it might be the saddle he wants to get rid of, not you!). You've probably also ridden the horse with imaginary fears—one that reverts to his prairie instincts and expects a mountain lion behind that bush at the edge of the woods.

How Two Minds Meet:
The Mental Dynamics
of Dressage

{2.1} **Below:** By nature, horses are herd animals, and even highly trained horses retain these herd instincts. Successful riders understand the herd mentality and utilize their horses' natural patterns of behavior.

{2.2} **Right:** As part of the herd mentality, horses inherit the need to look out for danger. When your horse trusts you as his rider and accepts you as his leader, he'll probably turn to you when he's anxious instead of reverting to flight.

19

WHAT TO DO
– The Mountain Lion –

AS most riders know, dealing with the imagined mountain lion takes patience and a proactive plan (fig. 2.3). When the scary place is approaching, gently flex your horse away from it so he doesn't need to face his fears. Then leg-yield, shoulder-fore, or shoulder-in past the offensive place.

If you are not an expert and don't know how to do these movements, that's okay. Help him to look away from the scary spot and use your leg on the same side to put him into the opposite rein. That is, if the scary spot is approaching on the right, use your left leg and rein, and move him forward and into the right rein.

Try to keep the rhythm, which is a form of comfort and balance for him. Praise him when he's brave. Over time, take him to places where he will see new sights, and manage to give him a good experience every time. Help him feel that he's brave. ●

● {2.3} When your horse reverts to his herd mentality, it's sometimes difficult to empower yourself to be the leader. Flex him away from the imaginary danger and push him sideways into your outside rein. Even if you're not an expert, you can help prevent him from stiffening and running away.

Emotionally, horses are innately as different as people are, or as dogs are. Some are friendly, self-assured, and trusting like a Labrador; some are scrappy like a Jack Russell Terrier; others are insecure and unreasonably fearful. But unlike dogs who love you no matter what, horses require that you earn their affection.

When horses are wronged, they certainly don't come back for more like dogs often do. They're closer to cats on the spectrum of showing positive emotion. They might, in fact, *feel* love, but they don't express it like dogs. Horses are matter of fact

How Two Minds Meet:
The Mental Dynamics
of Dressage

when it comes to what they like and what they don't like. They're more apt to show their fear than their positive responses. As a trainer working on gaining their trust, you try to reverse this trend. In the face of a fearful situation, a trained horse ideally turns to his rider for direction.

● Leadership on the Ground

Being the leader isn't always as simple as it sounds. Some horses wander aimlessly and don't act as if they want to follow you. Others are pushy, and they don't appear to see you as the leader, either: they invade your space and don't seem to want to be a follower. A horse might not be safe and trustworthy; you need to find a way for him to accept your leadership so you can trust him. Trust has to go both ways.

★ Try This

Let's talk about handling. Specifically, let's talk about leading, loading, and longeing—all of which involve the same physical and mental skills. There are entire books written about handling horses. Read them, but in the meanwhile, work on these principles.

Exercise: Respect My Space

In the herd, your horse was not allowed to crowd other horses. Teach him that he's not allowed to crowd you either. Begin with the right equipment. Horses who never need to be reprimanded are ones who have been taught how to carry themselves in their own space and respect the space of their people.

The aids provide a comfortable and invisible "box" within which he is balanced and can "play."

Teaching your horse to respect your space usually involves a whip that helps him manage to keep his body in his own space. He should learn to step calmly away from or forward from a light whip aid. Use a cluck at the same time as the whip, and he will eventually associate the cluck with the command to "go." Use the whip *as little as possible but as much as necessary,* and it will be effective. In time, you can, ideally, use it as gently as a paintbrush (fig. 2.4), but getting to that level of sensitivity takes training (see sidebar on Building Sensitivity, p. 24).

Teaching him to respect your space also involves a halter and a chain-lead shank that, once again, should be used *as little as possible but as much as necessary.* I recommend using the chain because it prevents pulling, which can damage the horse's very sensitive poll—the part of his spine that connects the head to the rest of his spine. The poll is a part of your horse's body that you don't want to have discomfort or dysfunction. The chain works on his nose. You don't often see noses that have been damaged by a chain, but there are, sadly, plenty of damaged polls.

21

{2.4} Teach your horse to carry himself in his own space and respect your space.

How Two Minds Meet:
The Mental Dynamics
of Dressage

When you want your horse to slow down or stop, engage the chain *as little as possible but as much as necessary*. Use your voice at the same time, saying "Whoa," which he probably understands. Soon the chain will become unnecessary. Then, instead of balancing him between the whip and the chain, he stays lightly framed and balanced between the cluck from behind and the halter or the whoa in the front.

Ask yourself, *Where are his feet?* Let your horse have the freedom to put his body where he wants, but you must gain control of where his feet are. This is an easy way to "draw the line."

- **Ask him to take a step back.** The rein-back is counter-intuitive to horses, but it will help you gain control of his feet.

- **Build a simple maze.** Make it moderately challenging, and he'll enjoy maneuvering his feet through it with you (fig. 2.5).

If your horse is slow, you'll need to use the whip and cluck more than the halter, and if he's a bully, you'll need the halter and maybe the

{2.5} Once your horse can be led reliably, help him manage his body parts by stepping through a maze. This will bring you both to a higher level of communication.

23

part one / chapter 2
Leadership and Freedom—Meeting
Your Horse's Herd Needs

Building Sensitivity

Carrying the whip and using a chain are a responsibility and the ability to use them as little as possible gives the rider maximum effect. But you only get to that level of sensitivity by using them as much as necessary when the horse is learning.

The concept of using the whip as "a whisper, a light tap or a strong tap" began many years ago with the former Chief Rider of the Spanish Riding School Karl Mikolka. The idea is to apply minimal use of the whip—just a whisper so that you can feel your horse's hair with the tip of your whip—and expect a result. That expectation is important because your horse will soon rise to that occasion, and you want to be open to rewarding the moment. If your "whispering whip" is ignored, you will apply a "light tap," and again, expect a response. If your "light tapping" is ignored, you'll give him a "strong tap" to demand a response. Then—and this is most important—you must reward your horse for his response and return to the whispering whip, which will probably be answered readily. Praise him again. Keep this principle in mind with all your aids, and attune your horse to the lightest aid. The system is to use your aids "as little as possible but as much as necessary." ●

chain more than the whip. When he learns to go where you want, you hardly need either. Under saddle, the rules are the same, and he stays lightly framed within the aids of the leg and the hand. The aids provide a comfortable and invisible "box" within which he is balanced and can "play." It all begins with leading.

Exercise: Ask Your Horse Questions

It's like a game. If you're asking the questions, then you're the leader.

Ask him, "Can you step away from this very light whip aid?" If not, tap him. Did he step away? If not, tap him more strongly so he understands.

Then, it's very important that you go back to the very light whip aid. Reward him and he'll be responsive to a whip that's used like a paint brush. Did he learn? He should walk next to your right shoulder.

Ask him: "Can you go? Can you stop? Turn right? Step back? Step away from me? Halt. Can you flex right? Left?" Notice his tail, his ears, and his facial expressions. Don't wear sunglasses because your eyes communicate by giving and taking information. Be open to communicating with him on a more meaningful level.

Exercise: Loading, Longeing, and Long-Lining Games

Horses who lead well also load well. They follow you—wherever (fig. 2.6). Horses who load well also longe well. They know how to step away from you to make the circle larger and stay properly oriented to you. If the horse doesn't know how to step away from your whip,

● {2.6} **Left:** If your horse has learned to be led and will follow you anywhere, he should trust you to lead him into the trailer. Leading and loading are the same skill.

● {2.7} **Above:** Wilfried Gehrmann of Germany is an expert at handling horses. Here he balances Dresden Mann beautifully on the longe line.

25 ____

● {2.8 A & B} Long-lining is an extraordinary training tool. It eases the transition to work under saddle because it makes horses very rideable. In these photos, Wilfried Gehrmann long-lines German Olympian Ingrid Klimke's mount Dresden Mann before she rides him in the arena.

Leadership as a Mentality

Most riders ideally have a regular trainer or coach, but sometimes there's just no one to help. There once was a capable young rider who had always been in full training at her barn. When she went away to college, she took her horse with her and was without help for several months. When she returned to her home stable for the holidays, everyone was somewhat surprised to see that she was riding better than ever, and her horse looked fabulous.

"How did you do it?" asked her trainer. "Well," said the young rider, "I always just assumed I was right. Then I figured that when I got my next lesson, I might learn how to improve something, in which case I would make a change in what I was doing. But when it was just me and the horse, I assumed I was right."

Your horse is a herd animal, and that horse's need for a leader was fulfilled. The young rider was unwavering in her leadership skills, and her clarity gave him confidence. She had the quiet courage of her convictions and a trainer's mentality. ●

a little "stomp" in his direction will usually set him back. You're asking for even more space than you had when you were leading, and he just needs to understand that. When your horse is learning to step away, he may actually be afraid of that little "stomp," and he may run away from you. In this case, it's vital that you go out to him at the end of the longe line, ask him to halt, and praise him until he relaxes. He will audibly sigh. When he's convinced that you're his friend, try it again. You may have to teach him about stepping away from you several times. Be patient.

Longeing is all about orientation, which means he gives you the right amount of space, not lagging behind you and not running away from you. He must go out to the end of the line wherever that is—a 15-meter circle or a 20-meter circle. However long you make the longe line, that is where he goes, and he tracks left or right in the gait of your choice (fig. 2.7).

Horses innately know that you're the leader when you play leading, loading, longeing, and long-lining games with them. It's remarkably similar to riding. The horse that is a bully or a laggard will suddenly love being the follower, but it will take effort on your part. Your aids (in this case, the whip/cluck, the chain/halter, or longe line and your voice) keep him balanced and able to move with ease; horses that are long-lined are far more confident and balanced when the rider gets on (figs. 2.8 A & B). His energies flow with yours as in a dance—even if it's not such a pretty dance to begin with. With clarity and consistency, it will become pretty. As your aids are able to shape him, he comes into a balanced posture, which makes him relaxed and comfortable in his own skin.

● Leadership Under Saddle

Under saddle, horses definitely have remnants of the herd mentality. They still need a *leader*, they still appreciate a sense of *freedom,* and they don't mind being told where to go and how to get there by the leader. When you're in the saddle, that's you. You're the leader.

Active Aids and Passive Aids

Your aids are active when you ask a question, and they are passive when you listen and give him time to respond. *Active aids* establish the rider as the leader. They say, *Let's do this now!* On the other hand, *passive aids* provide a moment of freedom for the horse and also time for the rider to listen for the horse's reaction. The passive aids also say, *Good! This is what I want!* Although the passive aids do not establish you as a leader, they do make you the kind of rider the horse *wants* to follow.

When a rider is just learning, she will be unable to be passive, and, therefore, unable to be completely effective with her active aids because she gives so many unintentional aids. At that point, the rider's primary focus is learning to be a passive follower. She can best acquire this ability to follow and be passive on the longe line with a horse controlled by the instructor. Later she can learn how to use active aids that come from a quiet place.

With passive aids, the rider is not only listening but also allowing her horse the freedom to physically carry himself and make the mental choice to obey her wishes. His feeling of freedom

Under saddle, horses definitely have remnants of the herd mentality.

gives the outward appearance that he's performing of his own accord. This is what makes him look beautiful on the "outside" as well as happy on the "inside." It has been said that a great leader is one whose followers don't feel they're being led. Well-trained horses don't feel subservient. They're partners in the dance.

Trustworthy Leader

Horses are usually happy when they're ridden by a *trustworthy leader.* To be seen as the *leader,* you don't need to be aggressive, but do need to be able to stand your ground sometimes and establish yourself as the leader by being task-oriented (see exercises on p. 29).

The horse knows who the leader of the dance is in the first 10 seconds. So if you get on and wander around like the lost tribes of Egypt, misaligning his neck while chatting with your friends, *he* is the leader and he knows this. In the absence of a leader, some horses become worried and others are happy to wander around, but don't expect them to be tuned in to you all of a sudden when you're done chatting.

To be seen as *trustworthy*, you need to be consistent, clear, kind, and fair. This doesn't mean you spoil your horse. You can be quite challenging as a trainer and still be consistent, clear, kind, and fair. Consistency and clarity require the physical skill and ability to follow the horse precisely, then to give exactly the same aids for the same request every time. The ideal trainer expects exactly the same response to these same aids.

Even if you aren't skilled enough yet to be even close to the ideal trainer, concentrate on the goal of being consistent, clear, kind, and fair with the intention of being successful. It will help. When you concentrate with the right intention, your horse will understand less-than-ideal aids, and both of you will improve.

There is a German word: *consequent*. I'll discuss this word more later (see p. 65). But for now, know that it's an adjective that describes the consistently clear aids from which the rider expects very precise responses *as a consequence of* those precise aids. With this consistent clarity, the horse understands and is obedient to your aids, you reward the horse for his positive responses, and trust is built.

You establish yourself as the trustworthy leader in the beginning of your ride, but that doesn't mean you go right to work. When you get on, your horse needs at least 10 or 15 minutes of walking to lubricate the joints and warm up the muscles. When this walking is the daily routine, he comes to expect the relaxation and looseness it brings to the work session.

The benefits of his comfortable attitude are far-reaching.

(see p. 65)

★ Try This

Be a task-oriented leader. During your walk session, you may be able to just relax and enjoy a trail ride, but carry yourself well as you ask your horse to carry himself well. Some horses require you keep them busy, in which case you can give them little tasks. These simple little tasks immediately put you in the position of being the leader.

Exercise: Be Task-Oriented

Here's an example of how you can be a task-oriented leader at the walk:

1. Free walk on a long rein across the diagonal (assuming it's safe to ride with no rein contact), then put him together in a medium walk with light contact before the corner and ride a very shallow corner. Don't go deep into it but be aware of the amount of consistent bend you have.

2. On the next long side, practice your turning aids: Turn onto a line that is parallel to the short side and then turn again onto the other long side. Practice going left and right. Confirm your turning aids so your horse understands them before you even go to trot.

3. From medium walk, when you're parallel to the short side, halt, and ask your horse for a turn-on-the-forehand. This will confirm the aids for the half-halt because in both the half-halt and the turn-on-the-forehand, the rider asks the hindquarters

29

{2.9 A & B} Ask your horse to flex left by bending your wrist so that your knuckles face your belt buckle (A), then slowly straighten and flex him right (B). This flexion exercise teaches your horse how to stabilize his body and respond to your rein aids appropriately.

to activate at the same time that the rein aids are saying, Wait a second. These are somewhat contradictory aids, and they require some level of sophistication. You can confirm this skill before you even trot.

4. In medium walk, from the short side, turn onto the three-quarter line and do a shallow leg-yield to a specific destination: a letter or, when you're not in an arena, a fence post or tree.

5. Halt and gently ask him to flex left by bending your wrist so that your knuckles face your belt buckle, then slooooowly straighten and flex right (figs. 2.9 A & B). Keep your hands in front of the saddle. The common problem of bending your

The Limits of Leadership

When a new mare came into my daughter Jennifer Baumert's life, she was eager to listen to everything the horse had to say. She wanted to get to know the new mare, so her first time in the saddle, she asked lots of questions: "How are you? How do you feel today? What's your opinion of this and that?" The first day went well. Despite some basic connection issues, Jennifer felt she had a great rapport with the mare. The next day, Jennifer was armed with an agenda that she felt was a positive and appropriate plan. But the mare could feel Jennifer's determination and felt threatened. In the past, other riders hadn't been very kind and fair leaders, so the mare was immediately concerned about her rider's position as leader. Jennifer was surprised that the mare suddenly became defensive.

Individual horses determine the limits to your leadership, especially when it comes to mares and ponies. There is a saying, "You ask a stallion, tell a gelding, negotiate with a mare, and pray with a pony." Some might say you submit a 10-page request form to a mare!

The bottom line is that all horses are different. When, over time, Jennifer's mare grew to trust her, she was a very willing partner, but Jennifer always respected her leadership limitations—always made small talk during the warm-up to check on the mare's basic comforts.

Mares have a reputation for being opinionated because they have a keen sense of fairness. Ones with a history of less-than-ideal riding are particularly guarded. It isn't simply about gender and temperament but about history and whether the horse is trusting or not. ●

---

arm causes the horse's neck to bend. This flexion exercise teaches your horse how to respond to your rein aids appropriately. If your horse is like most, he will mistakenly respond by misaligning his hindquarters when you use the rein. Can he do it without moving his body all around? He should react to your rein aids with his head and neck, not by backing up or swinging his haunches left or right. If he doesn't understand, patiently correct him. This takes time.

6. Repeat the free walk frequently so he uses all the muscles in his body, and then repeat the transition to medium walk to see if he can continue to use his whole body.

7. Be sure, in all walk work, that his nose reaches out on the forward moment and your hands follow. In walk and canter, horses use the neck to balance. Within every stride, he has a forward-reaching moment and a moment of coming back. His nose shouldn't come back on the forward moment.

31

When Your Horse "Lets You In"

● {2.10} When the horse "let's you in" by giving you access to his body and mind, it's a big deal.

Through consistency over time, your horse comes to trust you, and he "lets you in." That is, you have access to his body physically (because he accepts your aids), and he lets you into his mind (by communicating). When a horse "lets you in," it's a big deal because his innate claustrophobic tendencies make him want his own physical space. When you and your horse are "one," you share physical and mental energy. "Two spines align" and "two minds meet." It's a very big deal indeed. ●

How Two Minds Meet:
The Mental Dynamics
of Dressage

● Lead the Conversation

Attention to and concentration on all the little details establish you as the leader of the dance. There is an endless supply of exercises and tiny challenges you can master to increase understanding in the walk. They involve the skills of "go, stop, and turn."

The same is true of trot and canter. You're the leader when you initiate a conversation by asking for something with your aids. That's like your horse's "phone" is ringing. You expect him to pick up and respond.

All constructive and enjoyable conversations are two-way, so you need passive aids and active aids, and you need to be the initiator. You need to be proactive rather than reactive. You don't want to be in the position of saying, "*Don't do that,*" because, as you know, your horse doesn't understand negativity.

You need your communications to be positive. Tell him what you want rather than what you don't. Give him fun little challenges. Make wise left-brained decisions and then be present—in the *now*—to communicate with your horse. Remember, your aids are active when you ask a question, and they are passive when you listen and give him time to respond. You're the leader—the **trustworthy** leader.

● Freedom Through Balance

Another remnant of your horse's herd mentality is his appreciation for freedom. In fact the feeling of freedom is part of the "Spirit of Horse," which is part of his allure. It's why Pegasus and the unicorn

You need your communications to be positive. Tell your horse what you want rather than what you don't.

were invented by man in the first place. It's why therapeutic riding is so very therapeutic. It gives every rider a taste of the freedom that is the essence of the "Spirit of Horse."

Horses in the herd are naturally balanced, but when a rider gets on, this balance is compromised, and it's the rider's job to help the horse balance under saddle. Once in balance, he regains that feeling of freedom, which makes him happy. Out of balance (either in nature, in hand, or under saddle), there is a degree of discomfort and negative tension that manifests itself in mental tension, anxiety or confusion, and to some degree in a physical fight-or-flight response.

Horses hate to be out of balance, and under saddle, they are unable to balance without the help of a rider. The rider must learn how to be balanced herself, and use her aids to help the horse balance. Then a horse's job is physically and mentally as easy as possible. In balance, he can be free of tension. When he is uncomfortable, he can't learn, and if he can't learn, you can't train him. It's that simple. When he's in balance, he feels free and the rider is in control. You're in the land of all possibilities.

33

Riders spend years learning how to balance themselves and their horses, and then they spend their remaining years refining that balance.

When you ride your horse in balance, the work makes him stronger and suppler instead of tiring or stressing him. The goal of *When Two Spines Align: Dressage Dynamics* is to help riders develop their horses in a comfortable balance (see p. 35 to see the three ways to physically balance your horse). Physical comfort enables the horse to be mentally balanced and comfortable. Then energy flows through the horse's entire body in the right way, and his back swings. You can see it, or under saddle you can feel it, and you know the horse is connected, supple, and loose.

● The Leader Provides Balance

Just as you balance your horse in hand between the whip and the halter, under saddle you balance him between the seat/leg aid and the hand. Your seat, leg, and rein aids keep him in that comfortable, invisible box where he's balanced so he feels free and athletic. He is in front of the leg (willing to go), on the seat (willing to be supple and adjustable), and to the hand (willing to be directed and able to stop).

When the horse falls out of balance, the average rider might make the mistake of being passive and *re*active instead of being *pro*active. Her unbalanced horse needs to be quietly but actively interrupted with exercises that help him regain his balance. Remember that the passive aids tell the horse that everything is perfect. Often the balance is *not* perfect. Horses are innately inclined to use their front legs more than their hind legs, which makes them strong in the hand and inaccessible

behind the saddle. This feeling is uncomfortable for both horse and rider. Everything *isn't* perfect, so you need active aids to put your horse in balance. You need methods to balance your horse.

● Three Ways to Balance Your Horse

Think very objectively about balancing your horse. There are only two ways he can *lose* his balance: laterally (left to right and right to left) and longitudinally (front to back and back to front). Laterally, your horse can fall left or fall right. On a circle, he can fall in or fall out. Lateral balance is always improved by doing shoulder-fore. It's that simple. When your horse can do shoulder-fore left and shoulder-fore right, he is balanced laterally.

Longitudinally, your horse can lose his balance by going forward too much or not forward enough. There are two exercises that balance your horse longitudinally between the "Go" aids and the "Whoa" aids: half-halts and transitions. It's that simple. None of it is easy, but it *is* simple. Remember the simplicity and remember that your horse can't balance without you! Even the best-trained horses in the world require a rider who helps them to balance. Half-halts, transitions, and shoulder-fore are your means to perfect balance.

1: Shoulder-Fore

You can balance your horse laterally with shoulder-fore. If you have the luxury of being able to ride straight toward a mirror, it is easy to get immediate visual feedback. If not, find a friend who can watch and give you feedback. Your helper doesn't need to be an expert.

{2.11} When your horse can do shoulder-fore left and shoulder-fore right, he is straight and balanced laterally. Here, Jennifer Sekreve of the Netherlands is riding San Siro.

Begin by asking for shoulder-fore right (fig. 2.11):

1. Bend your inside (right) wrist (so your knuckles face your belt buckle) and ask your horse to flex very slightly to the inside (right). Flexion right will create a very slight arc of the neck to the right. Keep your hand in front of the saddle, so you don't bend the neck with your rein aid.

2. Use your primary diagonal aids: inside leg to outside rein, (in this case, right leg and left rein) to ask your horse to narrow his inside right hind leg to step under your seat. You or your helper should see him step with his right hind foot into the space between his two front legs.

3. Use your secondary diagonal aids: inside rein and outside leg, (in this case, left leg and right rein) as needed to retain the slight flexion to the inside and prevent your horse's outside hind leg from stepping out—as it will be inclined to do. You or your helper should see the outside hind aligned behind the outside fore.

As you try this for the first time, don't worry if you and your horse fall haphazardly left and right. Be persistent and patient. You will get it, and your horse will start to meet you halfway when he realizes that this is the way to balance. Eventually, shoulder-fore will stabilize your horse's balance and straightness. Change directions because you must be able to ride shoulder-fore in both directions.

This is not an "exercise." Shoulder-fore is simply riding straight. You should use shoulder-fore at all times.

2: Half-Halts

Remember that horses are innately inclined to use their front legs more than their hind legs, which puts them out of balance.

The horse's too-active forehand is his pulling engine. This engine is important, but when it does too much pulling, the hind end becomes like a trailer tagging along behind a tow vehicle (fig. 2.12 A). Because

your horse naturally wants freedom of the forehand, he prefers to use this front-end engine more than his hind engine. He doesn't realize that overusing his forehand puts too much weight on it, which actually reduces his freedom.

As soon as the horse takes a step with the front end without bringing his hindquarters along the same amount, he becomes a bit long in his frame, hollow in the back, and unpleasant in the hand. The horse needs you to explain that *real* freedom from improved balance comes when he uses his hind end more and his forehand less.

That's why the aids for the half-halt work! They say, *Wait a second!* to the forehand, and *Come on, get to work!* to the hindquarters.

You want your horse's hind-end engine to push your horse along, which creates a connection from his hindquarters to the bit (fig. 2.12 B). The pushing engine has to step under the center of gravity and create enough energy to get *all the way* from the horse's thrusting hind leg, through the horse's topline, to his reaching poll, and to the bit. Then it can lift and free the front end—your ultimate goal.

When the enthusiastic front legs carry the forehand away from the hindquarters, the horse disengages. In addition to the horse's natural tendency, his reaction to the rider's leg is sometimes to

● {2.12 A & B}
The hindquarters, when left to their own devices, sometimes act like a trailer being towed by the forehand (A). Half-halts help the hindquarters become the driving force, which has the effect of lifting the forehand (B).

37

Most horses, because of their inherent need to feel free, hate feeling claustrophobic, so riders need to take care that the aids don't make the horse feel trapped. Often horses back off when the aids get too tight, and the rider, instead of getting a "Go" response gets "Whoa." In this case, the rider has to ask for "Go" in a different way. Perhaps a snappier, quicker aid instead of a pressing or squeezing influence.

Give an aid and then take it away. Soon after the aids are active, they need to become passive. It's a fine line. When you are too passive, your horse falls out of balance, and if you are not passive enough, the horse gets tight and he feels claustrophobic. Your challenge is to help the horse feel free while you retain control. There's only one way for your horse to honestly feel free, and that is by straightening and balancing him so he can carry himself—and you. A crooked, unbalanced horse has inevitable physical tension, which creates a certain amount of mental tension, confusion or angst—all of which translate into lack of freedom. ●

disengage (figs. 2.13 and 2.14). The croup goes up and the horse's hind feet step *away* from, instead of *toward* the center of gravity (fig. 2.15).

Half-halts require active aids and passive aids. Passive aids follow the horse very precisely. You follow the horse's mouth with your arms, follow the horse's back with your seat and follow the horse's rib cage with your legs. These passive aids are nearly invisible because they are "one" with your horse's movement. Learning to follow takes years of quiet, concentrated persistence. During that time, your skills gradually become automatic. You eventually learn to follow the horse's motion unconsciously. In the beginning, however, you need to follow your horse very consciously, and as the horse moves, the *now* moment changes constantly, so it takes concentration:

1. Your hands follow your horse's mouth, which requires supple shoulders and elbows. In the walk and the canter, he uses his neck for balance, forward and back, so following precisely requires skill. In the trot, his head and neck are relatively stable, but it still requires skill to keep a consistent rein contact with relaxed hands that don't interfere at all. Your horse should feel that you're completely one with the motion of his head and neck.

2. Your seat follows his back very quietly. The floor of your seat is the triangular surface between the two sitting bones and the pubic bone. Your hips are flexible, so the floor of your seat can follow very precisely. No digging or shoving! That gives unintentional and harsh seat aids that will be inclined to

{2.14} Left: Sometimes the horse's reaction to the leg is to disengage. That is, the croup goes up and the horse's hind feet step *away* from, instead of *toward* the center of gravity. Train your horse to engage his hindquarters when you use your legs. Ask him to step under your center of gravity.

{2.13} Below: Horses aren't generally happy when they are disengaged—even in freedom.

hollow your horse's back. Because your legs are balanced under you, you can make your seat as light or as heavy as you wish.

3. Your legs follow his rib cage. When the horse pushes off with his left hind leg, his rib cage swings to the right, giving your left leg a little place to be. Step down into that space. Then in the next moment, the same thing happens on the other side. It's important that your seat and torso not shift as your legs follow your horse's rib cage.

As you try to accommodate your horse's movement with your hands, seat, and legs, you're physically harmonious or "at one" with your horse, and your passive aids are ideal. It's very subtle and looks like you're very quiet because you are

{2.15} Teach your horse to engage his hindquarters by stepping under the center of gravity, pushing and carrying (engaging). Jennifer Sekreve is riding San Siro in shoulder-in.

How Two Minds Meet:
The Mental Dynamics
of Dressage

in concert with your horse. He will be appreciative, and depending on his sensitivity, he might be *un*appreciative when you're less than successful. Of course, none of us is perfect, but concentration always helps, and you will improve with time.

When the aids are passive, the horse feels free to carry himself and you. The most important expression of approval and appreciation is to honor the horse's body by not disturbing it. When you're finally able to follow, your ability to *not* follow enhances the clarity of your *active* aids. In other words, your active aids are more audible if they come from a passive place instead of a noisy place.

When do you use your passive aids? When the balance is perfect. When the moment is less than perfect, you *stop* following and give an aid—a half-halt aid—to improve the balance.

How to Half-Halt

The half-halt always means, *Balance under me.* The half-halt always asks the hindquarters to engage and the forehand to wait. The active aids go like this:

1. The hands stop following (in walk and in canter). In trot, the fingers close. (It's very important that they weren't tight to begin with!)

2. The seat and leg push into the fixed hand so the horse gets slightly compressed from behind and ridden to the hand.

3. The hands soften and become passive again.

Horses Make Us Great Leaders

Trainers who are extremely successful have learned to balance their horses both mentally and physically; they teach their horses skills within the limits of their physical and mental abilities and they allow the horse to carry himself and feel free. Great riders have honed these skills.

Imagine, just for a second, if responsible leaders applied these skills to people in their everyday lives. What if managers of people utilized these same skills? What if they put their employees in balance, taught them skills that made them physically and mentally strong and then allowed them the freedom to be all they could be? What if all parents and teachers did that for children? Wow! Food for thought. When you think about it, horses teach us how to be great leaders. ●

41

Practice this. If you're not good at it, keep trying. It's simple but not easy, and when your horse starts to understand, the half-halt *will* work to create harmony and balance.

How often do you half-halt? As often as is necessary for your horse to remain balanced, which is usually quite often. The half-halt is brief but frequent, and your concentration needs to be there during each millisecond of the process. Your active aids send a communication to your horse and that communication establishes you as the leader. When the half-halt doesn't work, you soften, do it again and make it into a downward transition.

3: Transitions

A transition is a *change*. You say to your horse, *Let's do this now*. Transitions occur as a result of several half-halts. For example, the first half-halt says, *Let's get in a better balance*. The second one says, *Let's do something different*. And the third one says, *Do this*.

Half-halts and transitions improve communication by keeping both parties tuned in to each other. They not only make life fun and interesting for the horse but they also put the rider in the position of leader because she is the one asking the questions, "Can you do this? How about this? Can you do that?"

In the process, transitions serve the same purpose as half-halts. They balance the horse longitudinally between the leg and the hand—between the "Go" and the "Whoa" aids. The upward transitions reinforce the "Go" aid, and the downward transitions reinforce the "Whoa" aids. The horse thrusts and reaches with his hind legs in the upward transition and he engages, or carries weight on the hind leg that is grounded in the downward transition. As you practice transitions, the horse's balance improves:

1. The most basic transitions are those between two adjacent gaits: walk-halt-walk, trot-walk-trot, canter-trot-canter. Practice these transitions on a very precise 20-meter circle, and you will see your connection improve.

2. Then, on the same 20-meter circle, canter 10 strides, trot 10 strides and repeat. Counting the strides always makes a horse more prompt because he starts to anticipate your aids for a transition.

3. Change it up. When your horse gets good at that, try nine strides. Try it between trot and walk. These transitions will make your half-halts very effective!

★ Try This

Exercises for Balance

For a Strong Horse

When your horse is *too strong*, think up a simple exercise, preferably one that requires you to use *one* leg—because your horse might run away or get stronger in the hand from the use of both legs.

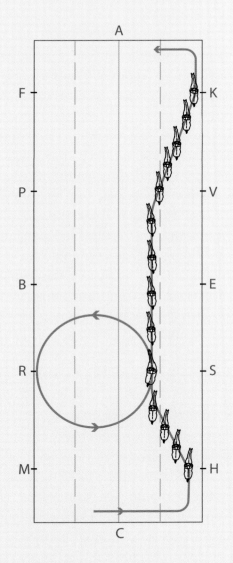

{2.16} Exercises for Balance—For a Strong Horse

Here's an example of an exercise that might help:

1. Track left and from a corner letter, flex right and leg-yield left to the quarterline.

2. At the quarterline, flex left and circle left 15 meters.

3. Go straight on the quarterline and leg-yield right to the far corner letter (fig. 2.16).

4. Change directions and repeat. Your leg aid will engage the horse's hindquarters and send him to the outside rein in one direction and then the other.

5. Now make up your own variations to suit your horse and his level of training, but have a plan. Your horse will become interested in your plan, and your aids will teach him to follow your plan. That's how you become the leader.

For a Lazy Horse

Maybe, instead of being too strong, your horse is inclined to be inactive. This horse also requires that his rider have a plan, and ideally a very interesting one. Think of a simple exercise, but this time, preferably one that requires you to use *both* legs. This horse needs to go forward, come back and turn.

1. Track left and from a corner letter, flex right and leg-yield left on the diagonal to the quarterline.

43

● {2.17} Exercises for Balance—For a Lazy Horse

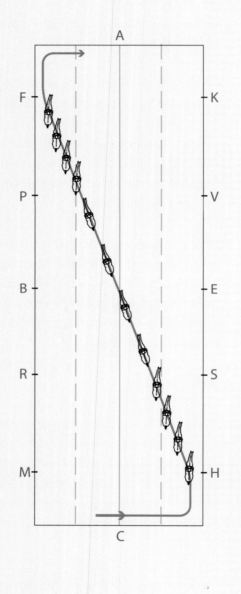

2. Straighten on the diagonal and lengthen the stride to the next quarterline.

3. Leg-yield on the rest of the diagonal to the corner letter (fig. 2.17). Do this in both directions.

Remember to switch between *planning* (which requires thinking about the future) and *feeling/concentrating* (which requires being in the moment).

If your exercises are successful, your horse will become mentally engaged and try to do them well. As an aside, he will become physically engaged, too. He will start to anticipate, which means you've won him over. He wants to play with you!

As more and more riders understand the physics of riding well, and can implement these physical principles by riding well, the mental and emotional aspects become more important. Indeed, equestrian contests are soon to be won or lost with the mind.

● Being a Responsible Leader

Horses remind us to be fair. If you're not fair and thoughtful about how you communicate, you might feel like you got what you wanted, but you didn't really. Harmony has a lot to do with trust, and trusting relationships have to be fair.

As your horse's leader, one of your important responsibilities is to honor his needs that are remnants of his herd mentality—to teach him to turn to you as a responsible leader and to help him balance so that he's comfortable and feels free.

Essential Information About Meeting Your Horse's Herd Needs

✓ **Horses are herd animals.** All successful horse-and-rider partnerships are based on understanding the herd mentality. Horses enjoy feeling free, and they are most comfortable when the rider assumes the role of leader.

✓ **Horses retain their feeling of freedom under saddle when the rider is able to** help the horse balance. The skills that help the horse balance are: shoulder-fore, half-halts and transitions.

✓ **Riders assume the role of leader first on the ground with the skills of leading, loading, and longeing.** Then those skills are utilized under saddle.

SUMMARY 2

"
A HORSE WITH GREAT INTELLIGENCE
IS QUICK TO UNDERSTAND, AND
THE HORSE WITH FINE CHARACTER
IS WILLING TO COMPLY.

How
Horses
Learn

3

It's difficult to quantify intelligence in the horse, but we surely notice the quick learner and the dull one. There are two aspects of equine learning that are sometimes difficult to separate: intelligence and character. A horse with great intelligence is quick to understand, and the horse with fine character is willing to comply. When you have an intelligent horse with fine character and a well conformed, strong body, you're indeed fortunate!

When horses are taught something new, their reactions and attitudes vary as much as they do in humans. Some horses think they know everything and are insulted when you explore new territory, *Oh my God, if you think I'm doing that at your every whim, you can forget it!*

It's interesting to note that this horse, once he catches on, is often very compliant. Some horses are intimidated, *Yikes! What are these poles on the ground? Where should my feet go?* And some are like the worker bee that just puts his nose to the grindstone and figures it out, *Wow! That was fun!* He's the one with great character who doesn't want to disappoint his rider.

A horse's intelligence isn't at all like ours. Because horses live in the *now*, they have no reasoning power, so they don't understand cause and effect in a rational, sequential way. They are, however, very trainable in cause and effect. Whether you're a beginner or an Olympian, your job is to help your horse understand the aids. For example, when you close your legs, your horse goes more forward. When you use one leg, he moves away from it. He must learn this, but he doesn't deduce it. He learns by *Repetition, Reward, Association, Clarity,* and *Persistent*

Monitor the horse's health, safety, and comfort with all the horsemanship skills available to you.

Consistency. These will be discussed one at a time on the pages that follow.

 Repetition

Anticipation is the positive byproduct of repetition. When you track right in trot and ask for a canter depart before a corner, a horse will be physically in a good position to do it. And when you do it in the same place three times in a row, you have a chance to refine the position and the timing of your aids. By the third time, your horse may predict or anticipate the canter depart and by then you have definitely refined his response to your aids. *Now* you can try it in a different place. We all know about the positive power of expectation, and anticipation is a close cousin to expectation.

Let's take the example of teaching your horse the rein-back. Stepping back is somewhat counterintuitive for the horse so it's often helpful to teach it from the ground by maneuvering his body (not his face) into a single step back. You might need to ask him to step sideways before you can successfully maneuver a step back.

The Prerequisites for Learning

AN unbalanced or uncomfortable horse cannot learn, and if he can't learn, you can't train him. It's that simple. Here are the prerequisites for learning:

- *You, as your horse's rider and leader, monitor his health, safety, and comfort with all the horsemanship skills available to you.*

- *You, as your horse's rider and leader, balance yourself in the saddle, learn to use passive and active aids, and use these skills to balance your horse with half-halts, transitions, and shoulder-fore to the best of your ability.*

Then we can talk about how the horse learns. ●

49

When your horse finally does step back, you **praise** him, and then you **repeat**. Now he **associates** stepping back with praise, and he understands what you wanted all along. Then when you repeat the request for a rein-back in the same way, it will be much easier to get the desired result. Next, you can try it while mounted, perhaps with someone on the ground asking in the same way the horse is accustomed. Although there is someone on his back, he will still anticipate the rein-back.

The horse will probably be pleased with himself for learning this new skill, so each time you halt under saddle, he might anticipate and do it when you *don't* ask for it. He might even step back after the initial halt in your dressage test. In this case, anticipation appears to work against you. You need to be a good sport about this because even though it will cost you a few points, the horse's intention was wonderful. He was anticipating what you wanted and expected you to be pleased.

Whereas you don't praise him for this effort, expressing displeasure would be a big mistake. Your horse quietly and patiently needs to become more cultured about rein-back and learn that he only gets praised when you *ask* for it. So quietly correct him by asking him to step forward when he has done a rein-back by mistake. In so doing, you've reestablished yourself as the *trustworthy leader*. First your horse learns *how* to do a rein-back, and then he learns *when* to do it, that is, only when you give him the aids for it.

The same is true with counter-canter and flying changes. The horse learns to do a flying change, and then will probably anticipate you asking for it again and be eager to repeat the change

The horse learns by Repetition, Reward, Association, Clarity, and Persistent Consistency.

because he knows how thrilled you were when he did it last time, and he's proud of his new skill. But your aids are very specific, and you must teach him to listen to the counter-canter aids and *not* do a flying change. As he becomes more experienced, he'll learn to discern between the two combinations of aids and know that you sometimes want him to do counter-canter instead of a flying change. Imagine how confused he would be if you were to punish him for doing a change when you wanted counter-canter.

It takes time for the horse to learn the difference between flying-change and counter-canter aids. He learns by quiet repetition with clear aids, reward, association and persistent consistency. He doesn't figure it out; he has no powers of reasoning. He only knows about the *positive now*. Horses anticipate as a result of repetition when they're mentally on your team.

Some people mistakenly avoid repetition because they don't want to "drill" their horses. However, horses need repetition because it's how they learn. They need to come to the point where they think, *Oh, I get it! THIS is what we're working on today!*

50

So when does repetition become drilling? Either when the horse doesn't understand the point, when he's just getting tired of the same old thing, or when the exercise is becoming physically difficult. When your horse understands what you want, he usually enjoys the exercise because he is able to do it better and better. In this case, it's not drilling. Horses enjoy repetition when it gives clarity to the lesson.

Your horse's first leg-yield might be very difficult. He may appear uncooperative, but when you think about it from his point of view, it's a ridiculous request. Why in the world should he flex right and go sideways to the left when he could go straight and get a better view of his destination? It really makes little sense.

After the third leg-yield, he has a clearer understanding of what you want, and you might leave it alone until tomorrow. After the fifth leg-yield, he might have become bored, tired, or cantankerous, and stopped learning.

Reasonable repetition develops "culture" because the horse comes to understand the lesson mentally. Once horses "get it," they can improve their abilities, add power, and even show off a bit.

★ Try This

Exercises That Use Repetition to Improve a Specific Quality

Well-conceived repetitive exercises can develop different qualities in a movement such as shoulder-in. Try these repetitive exercises:

Improve the *Bend* in a Shoulder-In

1. Begin tracking right in trot.

2. At M, circle right 10 meters, from M to B do shoulder-in.

3. At B, circle 10 meters; from B to F do shoulder-in; at F, circle 10 meters (fig. 3.1).

● {3.1} Exercise to Improve
the Bend in Shoulder-In

● {3.2} Exercise to Develop
"Throughness" in Shoulder-In

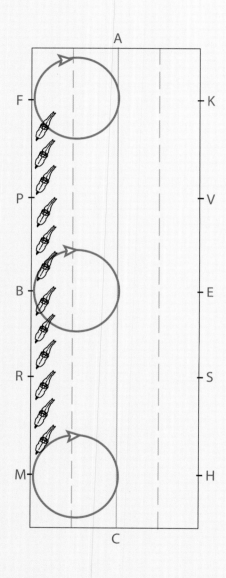

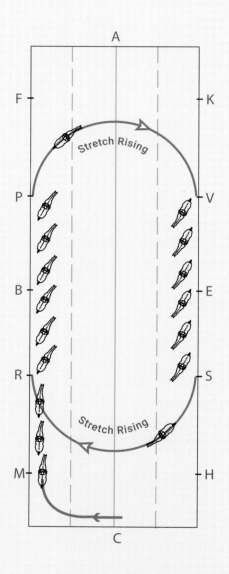

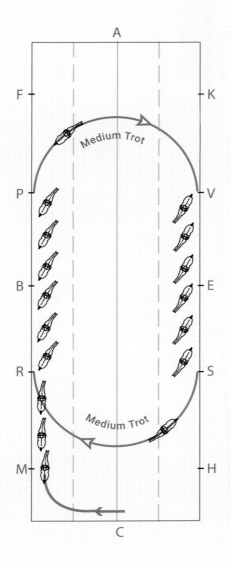

{3.3} Exercise to Develop Power in the Shoulder-In

The circles will improve your horse's bend and help to integrate this bend into the shoulder-in. Do this once in each direction and move on before he gets tired of too many circles.

Develop the Quality of *"Throughness"* in Shoulder-In

1. From R to P do shoulder-in; from P to V, do a half 20-meter circle, rising trot, allowing the horse to stretch.

2. From V to S, do shoulder-in; from S to R do another half 20-meter circle in rising trot, allowing the horse to stretch (fig. 3.2).

The stretches will improve your horse's use of his back in the shoulder-ins. Do this twice in each direction and move on.

Develop *Power* in the Shoulder-In

Repeat Exercise 2, but instead of doing a stretchy half circle, lengthen the stride to a medium trot on the half circles (fig. 3.3). The lengthening will add power to your horse's shoulder-ins. If you do these three exercises, your shoulder-ins will be supple and powerful. They will also improve your horse's medium trot, circles, and ability to stretch.

● Reward

Some riders think that sugar, carrots, and peppermints are the best reward, and their horses' reaction to these treats proves that there's some truth to the theory.

53

Make Collection a Positive Experience

What happens when there is a negative association with a critical part of horse training? That's often the case with collection, which begins at Second Level and is of vital importance in the subsequent training of horses. The compression required for collection can be associated with tightness, constriction, and lack of freedom that is spiritually counter to the horse's nature. Riders don't always know how to develop collection without restricting their horse's freedom. British superstar Carl Hester says that he sees riders all over the world who don't understand how to ride forward into collection. It's an extremely difficult concept.

For this reason, many horses and riders get stuck at Second Level, where collection is first required. Suddenly it really matters if the half-halts are ridden from back to front. Suddenly it really matters that the transitions actually engage the horse from behind. When you do it "a little bit correctly" you don't get "a little bit of collection." Instead, you get a little bit of collection when you do it well. And then, as the horse gets stronger, you'll get a little bit more collection. (See the exercise on p. 58 to help your horse feel free in collection.) ●

But on a more meaningful level, horses really want the same things we want. We may not think of the following as rewards, but these are what are most important to horses:

• **To be *comfortable*.** Does your horse's tack fit properly? Have his teeth been seen by a dentist? When you groom him, does he have any sore places? Do his eyes look bright and clear? Does he see a veterinarian regularly for wellness exams and vaccinations? Does he have protective equipment from whatever is needed in your area of the world? It might be fly masks, sheets, fly spray or protective boots for use during turnout. These examples are all a matter of good horsemanship, and these creature comforts add up to a reward. Remember, the uncomfortable horse cannot learn, and if he can't learn, you can't train him.

Horses anticipate as a result of repetition when they're mentally on your team.

- **To be *challenged* within reason.** Horses don't particularly like being bored any more than we do. Challenge your horse to tasks that may be a little stretch but won't be cause for anxiety (fig. 3.4). You wouldn't ask your First Level horse to do a canter pirouette, but you might be quite particular about the accuracy of his 10-meter circle or his leg-yield. (Read about the Comfort, Stretch, and Panic Zones on p. 71.) Choose the right time to challenge your horse. When he's physically in the right position to do more, you're likely to get a good response and a cascade of good results. Then the work is encouraging and rewarding to him.

- **To be *understood*.** When you know your horse will be afraid of the imaginary ghost in the bushes, meet the horse halfway by asking for a little shoulder-in or leg-yield past the scary place. Insist the horse keeps the rhythm, but make sure that he doesn't feel trapped and doesn't have to look at the scary place. Understanding also goes the other way. The horse's increased understanding of his work is a positive association. He loves feeling competent.

- **To have a *routine*.** Horses appreciate knowing what's going to happen next. It gives them confidence to know that they'll get their hay at a certain time (the same time as the others) and to know they'll be turned out at a specific time and place. Although there are times when the schedule varies, he often does best when it's consistent.

- **To be *appreciated*.** In your career, whatever it is, being appreciated ranks right up with your paycheck. Likewise, rewarding your horse goes a long way. As a reward for his efforts under saddle, he can look forward to a walk break and being praised. The best trainers pat the horse even when they are dissatisfied if they notice a slight improvement in the performance. It's very evident when you watch a horse who has been trained with reward next to one who has been punished.

These rewards are more important to him than the possible *dis*comfort that he inevitably feels from the process of getting stronger. It's the same as working out at the gym—the rewards need to be greater than the discomfort of those extra few repetitions. If they aren't, then you don't go back for more. The horse's challenging situations should be associated with the reward of being appreciated—whether it's with a lump of sugar or a pat.

Association

Cues help horses understand because of association. They associate an action, sound, or feel with a positive reaction or reward. They learn that

55

How Two Minds Meet:
The Mental Dynamics
of Dressage

{3.4} Horses enjoy a challenge such as cavalletti work. Be sure the cavalletti are set up correctly for the gait of choice. Spacing will vary depending on the size of your horse's gaits, but these are the averages: For walk, set them approximately .8 meters (2 feet, 7 inches) apart. For trot, set them about 1.3 meters (4 feet, 3 inches) apart, and for canter, set them about 3 meters (9 feet, 10 inches) apart.

application of the rider's legs means they should go forward and application of the reins means they should slow down. When you flex your horse to the right, the horse knows he will probably be tracking right (see *When Two Spines Align* for more information about flexion). When you put a little weight in the right stirrup, the horse learns he's going to turn right or canter on the right lead.

All these associations have a *natural* element to them. For example, a horse will naturally follow your weight in the same way that you naturally go right when a book on top of your head starts to fall that way. But soon the association between weight aids and direction starts to take on a mental understanding, and the horse becomes cultured about the weight aids. This predictability and understanding gives the horse a degree of mental comfort. And likewise, you are mentally comfortable, too, when you know what's going to happen next. There are many physical cues that become mental cues as soon as the horse learns them and understands because of association. For example, one great European rider taught his horse to piaffe when he scratched his withers. It was a trick, but a very wise one. This horse won the Grand Prix at the Aachen Horse Show at least once.

Association is about preparation. A half-halt rebalances the horse (see p. 36). It physically does that but it also mentally says, *Come to this place where we're better prepared to **do** something.* It's preparation for a change or a transition of some kind—a change of gait, a change of direction, or maybe a change in the length of the stride.

Effective trainers make their associations pleasant ones. The result of the aid might put the horse in a position in which he feels better. He might be in a better balance, he might earn himself a break, he might get a treat, or a pat for his efforts. These are all rewarding associations.

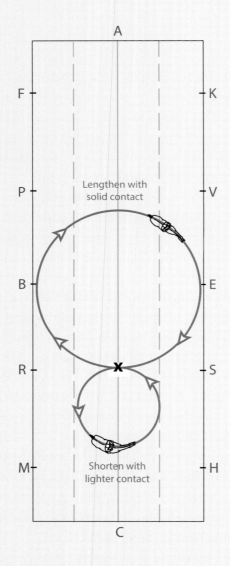

● {3.5} Exercise to Find Freedom in Collection

A

F — K

P — Lengthen with solid contact — V

B — E

R — **X** — S

M — Shorten with lighter contact — H

C

★ **Try This**

How can you help your horse associate collection with freedom? In collection, the horse's frame closes *from behind,* and he doesn't mind feeling compressed behind the saddle if he still feels free in front. Try to increase the effectiveness of your seat and leg, so your horse listens to that more than your hands. It's fine if you need to use your hands for half-halts but be sure to release, and concentrate on your seat and leg aids. Use them first and use your rein aids last.

Be sure to ride from back to front in your downward transitions and in your half-halts. In addition, follow these general guidelines:

- Be sure your horse is aligned in shoulder-fore so he is straight and stepping under your center of gravity. Alignment makes him able to be compressed in a supple way.

- Use your legs to encourage your horse to step to the bridle.

- At the same time, make your rein aids briefly set a boundary. They stop following the natural movement of the horse (in walk and canter), and/or you may close your fingers in trot. Your hands do not come back and shorten the neck.

- When your horse connects from back to front, your seat adds weight to the hind leg when it is on the ground so your horse becomes light in front, and so…

- …you can truly *give* in response to the horse's shorter strides and frame.

Reasonable repetition develops "culture" because the horse comes to understand the lesson mentally.

Practice this. It's simple but not easy.

When you feel that your horse is being *held* in front, you need to simply go back and improve the connection. When the connection isn't right, collection isn't possible.

To give your horse a feeling of freedom in collection you can use any exercise that includes lengthening and shortening the stride.

Exercise to Find Freedom in Collection

1. Begin on a 20-meter circle to the right (fig. 3.5). Lengthen the stride and try to develop a very solid contact in the lengthening.

2. As you approach the centerline, push your horse into shorter strides and circle left 10 meters. Try to make your contact lighter on this circle.

3. Next, return to the 20-meter circle to the right by lengthening the stride and trying to develop a very solid contact again. Keep thinking about shoulder-fore so your horse stays balanced between the inside leg and the outside rein. Your horse should stay committed to the bit. The lighter contact on the small circle should be a result of his engagement and self-carriage.

Horses aren't emotionally averse to compressing the hindquarters, but they are averse to having a tight neck and being held behind the vertical. Get accustomed to giving your horse freedom in collection.

● Clarity

Clarity is all about having clear aids that the horse understands. The best riders are able to be passive when everything is perfect and are able to give clear active aids when they want something different. Clarity also involves timing.

The horse's language, as explained in *When Two Spines Align*, is his rhythm. When you can give active aids in the rhythm of his gait, your aids are automatically well-timed. All riders, from beginner to the very best one, need to establish a common language with the horse. Then, within the rhythm, work it out with your horse.

Remember to do some work in walk. It's much easier to be clear at the speed of walk, and you can establish your language at that speed. Tell him what you want. Explain your aids for turning. Explain your aids for shoulder-fore. He needs to understand: *This amount of this aid means that.* No one can do this for you. Your trainer on the ground can make suggestions because she knows how to give the aids in a classical way, but she has no remote control buttons. *It's your aid.* You need to build a language of communication with

59

Why Some Horses Can't Be Re-Trained

Horses sometimes bring emotional baggage to the table because of their excellent memories of less-than-excellent experiences. Both their positive and negative memories influence and inform their present moment—and yours, too. If you're planning to buy or train a horse with negative emotional baggage, you may be able to bring him around to your way, but don't count on it. Just because you know what's wrong with him, doesn't mean you can fix it. Physically he may not recover from his past, and mentally, it may be hard to earn his trust, so you just don't know how that will come out. Many horses change and many don't, but horses have no moral code. They don't consciously make choices between right and wrong. The ones who have extraordinarily good character aren't that way because of an inner moral code that tells them to be good. ●

your horse. If you're only a beginner, do the best you can without apologies, and your skill will improve day after week, month, and year. You'll have good days and not-so-good days, but if you try to be consistent, your horse will be getting messages based on the same underlying system, so he will learn.

● Persistent Consistency

Consistency refers to the rider's underlying theory of riding that is systematic and has no contradictory aspects to it. Consistency also refers to the use of that theory over

{3.6} Molly O'Brien is riding the Lusitano stallion Telurico in a free walk on a long rein. Always pay attention to the quality of the walk, so your horse never practices a poor walk. He should feel like he is going toward the feed tub. Be consistent. In competition, the free walk is always a double coefficient movement.

time: that the rider uses the same theory minute to minute, hour by hour, day after day, after week, after month, after year. That's where persistence comes in. True consistency implies persistence. It goes on and on forever. The theory may evolve and become more sophisticated, but the attitudinal nature of it and the logic behind it doesn't change.

Consistency is every rider's friend and certainly every horse's friend. If your horse is allowed to do a poor free walk during a break, and he's falling left and falling right on Tuesday, how is he supposed to understand that when you're at a horse show on Saturday, he should do a free walk with good posture? He has no idea. If he only knows how to do one free walk—a balanced, elegant one—chances are enormous that he will do that one at the horse show (fig. 3.6).

For this reason, always do something with a name. You should be able to define what you're doing. For example, "I'm doing a working trot sitting with 15-meter bend. I'm doing a medium walk in shoulder-fore left. I'm doing collected canter, left lead." Know exactly what you're doing. Consistently. Again, you can achieve this consistency physically with practice, but there is also a mental aspect that you need to be neurotically focused on.

Inconsistency sometimes creeps in when a rider is afraid of making a mistake. In the process, she makes the biggest mistake of all—not telling the horse what she wants consistently. *When Two Spines Align* goes into great detail about how to help the horse carry himself in good posture. How often should the rider require that her horse carry himself with good posture? *All the time!* The horse will never learn if the rider isn't consistent about requiring this.

Consistency is every rider's friend.

Only when every stride is the same, can you ask for something different in a meaningful way. Only from a completely consistent canter can you ask for a balanced transition to trot or a balanced flying change. The horse needs to give you consistent working gaits, but you, the rider, must ask for that consistency and help him attain it. How? In balance. You're the leader of the dance, and a well-trained horse keeps doing that working canter, left lead until you say, *Now, I want to do a transition to working trot. Then I'm going to change direction and do…..*whatever you want. It's your story. You need to write it—consistently.

How Two Minds Meet:
The Mental Dynamics
of Dressage

Essential Information About How Horses Learn

✓ Horses who are unbalanced or uncomfortable can't learn so they can't be trained. Here are the prerequisites to learning:

1. *Monitor his health, safety and comfort with all the horsemanship skills available to you.*

2. *Learn to use passive and active aids, and use these skills to balance your horse with half-halts, transitions, and shoulder-fore to the best of your ability.*

✓ Horses learn by Repetition, Reward, Association, Clarity, and Persistent Consistency.

✓ Skilled trainers are able to make the development of collection a positive experience for their horses by riding back-to-front in all downward transitions so horses retain their sense of freedom.

SUMMARY 3

63

"
TRAINERS WHO ARE *CONSEQUENT* GIVE VERY
SPECIFIC AIDS AND EXPECT A VERY SPECIFIC
RESPONSE. CONSEQUENT TRAINERS KEEP
THEIR HORSES ON THE RIGHT ROAD.

4

The "Consequent" Trainer

CHAPTER

4

Remember the German adjective *consequent* (see p. 29)? The Germans say you should be *consequent* in your training. This means that when you give an aid, it should mean something very specific and you should expect a very specific answer from your horse. Horses can learn very specific aids and give very specific responses—for example, to lengthen the stride 2 inches.

Communicating clearly requires that you *know* exactly what you want. For example, the rider who wants a "lengthened stride" needs to know how long a stride she wants and exactly how she will ask for it. Do you want the stride to be a modest 2 inches longer? This a wise goal because it's better to lengthen the stride 2 inches and retain the integrity of how your horse uses his body instead of trying to do the maximum, only to have the horse go fast, lose his balance onto the forehand, and be unable to come back in balance. After your horse has mastered the 2-inch lengthened stride, 3 inches shouldn't be too hard; then 4 and 5 and so on. You can see where this is going.

In an effort to be *consequent,* the rider's mental expectation is a key element of success. Let's use "riding the corner" as an example. One hundred percent of horses try to cut the corner! After all, why should your horse go into the corner and balance through it? It's much easier for him to cut it, but the astute dressage or jumping rider knows that a corner or a turn is the place where you can help your horse become more balanced. Of course, it's also where the horse can lose his balance, which is what happens when he does the corner on his own. Let's take a look at a couple of situations that instructors see all the time:

How Two Minds Meet:
The Mental Dynamics
of Dressage

Does your horse think you're fun to be with?

- **Rachel** *is task-oriented and mentally committed to what she wants. She and her horse are tracking right in working trot toward the corner. Before the corner, Rachel half-halts in the shape of a 10-meter bend in preparation for the corner, but the horse doesn't "hear" her and he falls in. Rachel is surprised because she was expecting a balanced corner. "OOPS! Wait a second!" she instantly says to her horse with a series of half-halts that ask for a downward transition to a balanced walk. She then pushes him a bit with her inside leg over to the left in a little leg-yield. She trots again, and before the next corner she does a downward transition to walk, half-halts in the shape of a 10-meter bend and walks him through the corner in balance with bend to remind him of how he should respond to her aids. She retries it in trot.*

Bottom line: Rachel's horse didn't hear her aids, and he was immediately and kindly reminded of how to respond.

- **Michelle** *doesn't have quite so much confidence. She and her horse are tracking right in working trot toward the corner. Before the corner she half-halts in the shape of a 10-meter bend in preparation for the corner, but the horse doesn't hear her and he falls in. This is just the same problem that Rachel had, and Michelle may, in fact, be an equally skilled or even a better rider, but she blames herself and follows her horse by falling in both physically and mentally. She goes down a rabbit hole of wondering what she did wrong. She's no longer in the moment. She's no longer in any moment. Maybe my inside leg wasn't strong enough, she reasons, but his rib cage was bulging into it and that rib cage is stronger than my inside leg. The "moment" is long gone while Michelle is analyzing the situation.*

Bottom line: Michelle's horse has no idea he made a mistake by blowing through her aids.

In situations like this, riders can easily lose track of what they want, because they unwittingly compromise. To use the same example, the next time around, Michelle's horse keeps the line of travel, but he loses the bend. Michelle is pleased with that result, but the bend is actually the essence of the turn. Michelle lost track of what she wanted. Rachel's horse understood clearly so she got 100 percent of what she wanted.

To be fair, rider education and skill matter, and it's a good idea to do a little compromising in some ways. Make the task easier by making a shallower corner with, maybe, a 15-meter bend.

WHAT TO DO

– Take Advantage of Gravity –

UNGROUNDED

GROUNDED

When it comes to balancing through a corner—or balancing in any situation—your riding position is the primary factor that dictates your success. You are either the leader who can help your horse balance or the follower who, like the fictional Michelle (see p. 67), follows her horse out of balance.

I explained in *When Two Spines Align* that "the rider's feet serve as the extremely important bottom building block, and when the rider is vertically aligned, she has the same reference to the ground as when she is standing on it. This 'stance posture' is grounded to the earth and balanced according to the law of gravity."

When your leg is even slightly lifted, causing you to grip the saddle, you are in your horse's balance and you can't influence that balance or improve it. You're with the saddle, and the saddle will always be in your horse's balance. You will go where he goes—and that will be out of balance—because he can't balance on his own.

When the length of your leg is maximized and "grounded to the earth," your balance is independent from your horse and his saddle (figs. 4.1 A & B). You're stretched, with positive tension, which is very strong! When you're in this state of positive, grounded balance, your horse is inclined to come to your balance. It never pays to argue with Mother Nature. Gravity is free to those who remember to take advantage of it. ●

● {4.1 A & B} You want the length of your leg to be maximized and "grounded to the earth" so your balance is independent from your horse and his saddle. Liz Caron demonstrates how a rider can be ungrounded **(left)** and then grounded **(right)**. Her horse's posture improves dramatically when she is grounded.

How Two Minds Meet:
The Mental Dynamics
of Dressage

> *When a rider is consequent, she clearly explains what she wants to the horse, and then the horse understands and willingly complies with some level of specificity.*

It's wise to *knowingly* compromise by lowering the expectation and asking for less bend. But don't make the task easier by ignoring the essence of corner riding, which is bend.

Set realistic goals and achieve them in logical steps. It's not okay for a performance to be poor just because the *"What do you want?"* got squishy and unclear to the horse.

Remember, when a rider is *consequent,* she clearly explains what she wants to the horse, the horse then understands and willingly complies with some level of specificity. The results of Rachel will usually surpass the results of Michelle, even if Michelle has superior riding skills. Rachel is clear and *consequent.*

Know how to ask for what you want with active—but eventually subtle—aids that the horse understands. Then passive aids involve listening to your horse's response and either responding with gratitude for an appropriate response or responding with a clearer explanation of what you want when your horse's response was inappropriate.

● Engage Your Horse's Mind

When a horse engages his hindquarters, his hind-leg joints bend, his croup lowers, he carries more weight with those hindquarters, and as a result, the forehand becomes lighter. But engagement isn't just about the hindquarters. You also want to engage the horse's mind. Some horses are very smart and their minds can—and like to—carry "weight."

Halt-halts and transitions engage the horse mentally as well as physically. They say, *Let's do this now!* Riders who are leaders always have something interesting to say to their horses. But some riders complain that their horses don't pay attention to them. "He's not listening to me," is the common lament. Why isn't the horse listening?

Consider these ideas from your horse's point of view:

- **Are your messages clear?** Some riders may not be giving the message in a clear way because it is cluttered with unintentional aids or aids given at a time when the horse can't respond. That's often because the rider's position and her aids need to improve. For example, maybe she is unintentionally kicking the horse every step. That's not uncommon, but when she wants to give a leg aid, the horse doesn't "hear" it. Maybe the timing of the rider's aids is off because she's not in her horse's rhythm. Maybe her hands are unsteady so the horse is never completely relaxed in his topline and accepting the bit. Some riders, especially those who are very cerebral, think they are giving physical aids when they are not. Whereas a rider's aids are intended to be subtle, they might need to be louder if the horse doesn't hear them. When a rider's skills need to be honed, the best the rider can do is become aware of these shortcomings and work to improve them. When this is the case, a horse often somehow understands and meets the rider halfway.

- **Does your horse think you're fun to be with?** Some riders are just plain entertaining, and horses would agree. Others are boring because the language of their aids doesn't send an interesting message. They don't challenge themselves to be the leader, and are satisfied with going around and around (and around) in a less-than-ideal balance. Maybe they are not engaging their own minds. When you ask your horse interesting questions, every ride is like a game and he has fun. He looks forward to his rides, which challenge him.

- **Does he think you're fair?** Sometimes a rider may not have a pleasant message for her horse because the emotion behind it isn't positive. This rider may not be respectful of the horse's nature. She might not honor all his innate needs that were described earlier. Later (see p. 95). I'll discuss if the emotion behind a given message is a subcategory of fear or love? Fear and love can't reside in the same place. Ideally, the rider's emotion is a subcategory of love, and she is able to express her message—even a strong message—in a way that honors the nature of the horse.

- **Is he physically comfortable?** As you know, horses can't concentrate on the work if physical comfort is an issue. Check out his teeth, feet, eyes, muscles, and joints. Pay attention to clues that he may be giving you.

Some trainers say, "The way to a horse's body is through his mind." And others say, "The way to a horse's mind is through his body." Which is it? Either can be argued. It can be said that without physical harmony, there can be no mental and emotional comfort, which is why I wrote the book about the physical aspects of training first. But it is also true that you can't train a horse well unless you're his friend to begin with. Either way, the mind and the body are, indeed, closely aligned. Empower yourself to engage your horse's mind as well as his hindquarters.

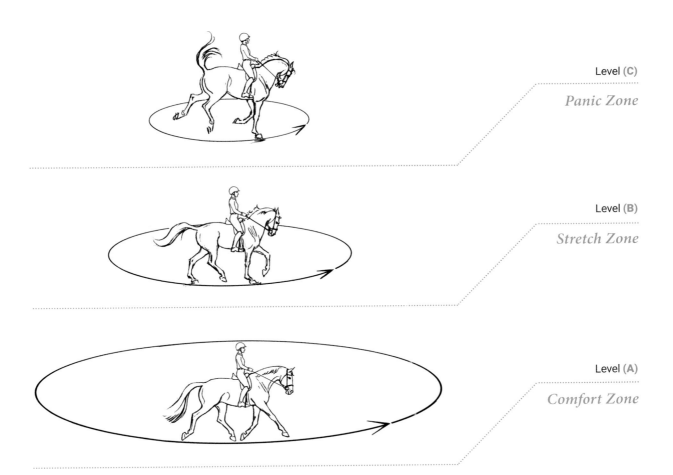

Level (C)

Panic Zone

Level (B)

Stretch Zone

Level (A)

Comfort Zone

● **The Comfort, Stretch, and Panic Zones**

Experienced riders are aware of the spectrum of emotions between comfort and extreme discomfort. These zones apply to both horse and rider (fig. 4.2).

• **The Comfort Zone** is exactly that. It's a place of comfort. Although learning doesn't take place in the comfort zone, it's an important place to spend time, gaining confidence, trust, and pleasure, so it's important to spend time there. Pleasure riders spend most of their time in the comfort zone, and perfectionists sometimes make the mistake of not venturing outside that comfortable place where the work is easy so the quality is high.

● {4.2} The Comfort Zone (A) is the place where horses and riders both gain confidence and trust, the Stretch Zone (B) is where learning takes place and new tasks might be physically or mentally challenging for horse or rider, and the Panic Zone (C) is a place where negative emotion is so high that learning can't take place.

71 _____

- **The Stretch Zone** is where learning takes place. It's a place where effort is required and may even be a bit of struggle, physically and mentally. There may be some anxiety over the learning of a new task. It might be uncomfortable but it's never dangerous or physically damaging.

- **The Panic Zone** is exactly that. In this place, the horse or rider is emotionally freaked out, and learning can never take place in this zone. The rare circumstance in which both horse and rider are in the Panic Zone is dangerous.

Some riders are inclined to stay in the Comfort Zone all the time. Learning doesn't happen there, but it's important to remember that learning isn't always the goal. Some riders need and want to ride for pleasure and relaxation. Horses in training need days when they're just going to have fun. They shouldn't feel that the saddle always means hard work because they should have fun under saddle, too.

The Comfort Zone is where horses often need to be. It's the place where previous learning is confirmed and horses build confidence, trust, and pleasurable experiences.

Some riders (the brave ones) can inadvertently put a timid horse in the Panic Zone. The ideal situation for training *horses* is with an experienced rider in her Comfort Zone while her horse is in the Stretch Zone. The ideal situation for training *riders* is with the experienced horse in his Comfort Zone while the rider is in the Stretch Zone. Hence the saying, "The old riders teach the young horses and the old horses teach the young riders."

> *It's easy to become overly serious, but an effortless, fun attitude is one of a rider's greatest assets.*

German rider Uta Gräf is an expert on fun, optimistic riding. Read her book *Uta Gräf's Effortless Dressage Program* if you want to understand more about how you can tap into your horse's desire to play. For Uta, that playfulness in the work is the key to lightness or responsiveness. It is also the key to success. Although most of us are very particular about correct technical riding, it would be mechanical and boring for both horse and rider without the positive attitudes that should accompany it. It's easy to become overly serious, but an effortless, fun attitude is one of a rider's greatest assets.

The primary responsibility of a competent rider is to keep her horse in physical comfort, and her secondary responsibility is to develop the horse and teach him. Everything from poor riding to ulcers to poor dental work and poor saddle fit to the full range of horsemanship concerns can cause discomfort and result in negative attitudes and emotions. Bad riding is, at least, uncomfortable and, at worst, torture. When the horse is balanced and "through," he's comfortable unless there's an underlying physical issue that has made work under saddle difficult.

How Two Minds Meet:
The Mental Dynamics
of Dressage

An experienced trainer develops her horse by playing on the edge of these comfort zones. If the horse is able to do a good lengthened stride on the short diagonal, she'll try it on the long diagonal. Was the horse able to stay engaged and relaxed? Can the horse do a free walk on a loose rein afterward? Next, the trainer tries the lengthened stride in the field on good footing. Can the horse still stay relaxed and engaged? Then she'll try it in the field going toward the barn. Is it still relaxed and engaged? Can the horse walk on a loose rein afterward? Horses enjoy little challenges that will increase their understanding.

When the rider honors and respects how the horse thinks and feels, she is aware of his fears, and she knows what he loves. She can help dispel his fears and help him love his work. When Olympian and top U.S. dressage coach Debbie McDonald teaches, she often tells the rider to "play" with the leg-yield or "play" with the shoulder-in. She wants her horses in training to feel that the work is fun. Her goal is to allow her horse's natural spirit to come through while retaining his physical balance and his mental interest.

summary of chapter 4

Essential Information About Being a Consequent Trainer

✓ Being "consequent" means that you can give very specific aids and expect a very specific reaction from your horse.

✓ Skilled riders are aware of their horses' Comfort Zone, Stretch Zone, and Panic Zone. They are conscious about giving their horses plenty of time in their Comfort Zone, and they use the Stretch Zone without panicking their horses.

✓ Ideally, horses feel their riders are fun, challenging, and fair.

SUMMARY 4

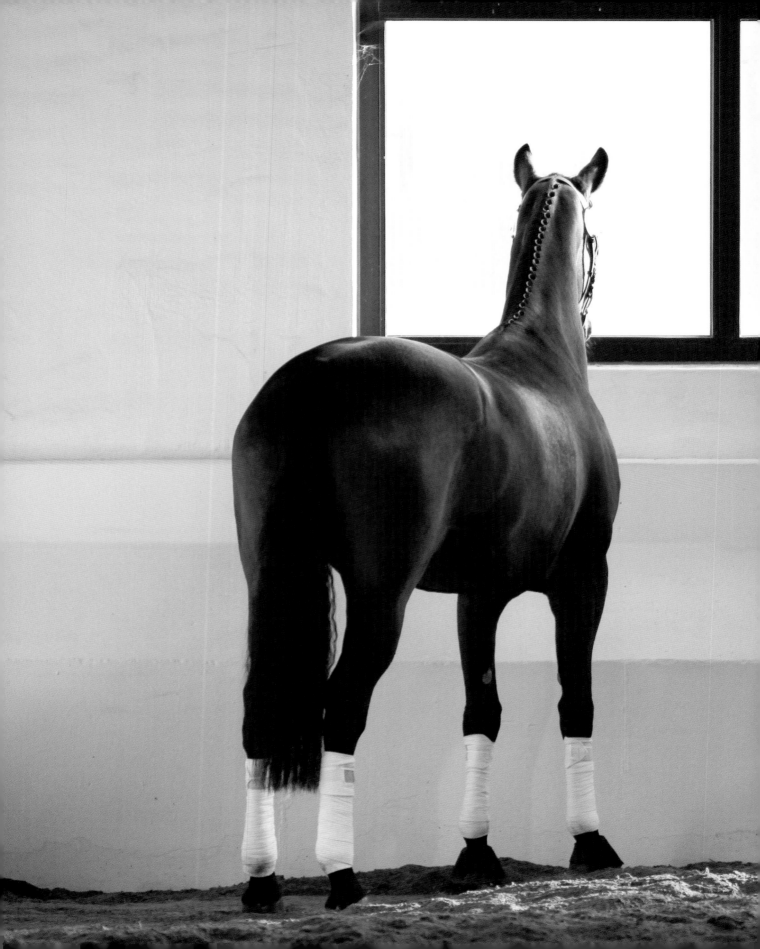

PART TWO

The Rider's Multiple Minds

> "HUMANS ARE THINKERS. WE LOVE TO FIGURE THINGS OUT, AND IN MOST ASPECTS OF OUR LIVES, WE'RE JUDGED BY HOW WELL WE THINK.

5

The Rider's Left Brain: Learning and Organizing Knowledge

5

Humans are thinkers. We love to figure things out, and in most aspects of our lives, we're judged by how well we think. The *thinking* mind is the *learning* mind, and life's contests often involve who can outthink whom, and who has the most knowledge, which is traditionally considered to be stored in the "left brain."

Humans are further judged on their abilities to solve problems. "Creative" problem solvers are able to tap into the "right brain," which is less orderly and has an ability to shake things up so as to visualize a different and potentially more useful order of things.

Although the logical, thinking, knowledge-accumulating left brain is only a part of the rider's mental capacity, it's an important part because it informs and influences the other dimensions of the mind. The left brain knows, for example, that the one-and-only board meeting of the organization that might buy your great new product convenes at 9:00 a.m. next Tuesday. The creative, often disorderly right brain has to acknowledge that reality, or it will not be able to present its creative, brilliant idea to the board.

The rider's logical-thinking left brain knows the date of the show, it knows the appropriate class and the time of that class. It knows all the rules, and over time, it has organized the horse's equipment, his feed and nutrition, his medications, his grooming tools, and so on. Beyond that, the rider intellectually understands the physical and mental needs of horses. She understands the basics and perhaps the finer aspects of how to ride horses, and has trained her body to do the best possible job in the saddle.

Your conscious mind can only concentrate and learn one thing at a time.

The thinking rider comes to the table (or the saddle) with a world of extremely important and detailed information that will send her down a successful path as a horse trainer. Some of the best equestrians in the world are compulsive learners who have been in the business for decades and can still say they learn something new every day. Carl Hester, Robert Dover, Denny Emerson, Jim Wofford, Lendon Gray, Kyra Kyrklund, and many others are extraordinary people and horsemen because they keep learning. They're still reading and attending conferences, always ready to learn more and quick to share their newest enlightenments. Almost all serious learners in the equestrian world are extremely generous with their knowledge and love teaching. They are, indeed, way ahead of the game and in the best position to maximize the success of the horses under their tutelage. These people are not only good at gathering knowledge, but also good at categorizing it, acting on it, and sharing it. It should be noted that knowledge isn't useful until you categorize it and act on it.

Let's look at how riders learn.

● Thinking and How Riders Learn

Your conscious mind can only concentrate on and learn one thing at a time. As soon as this skill is mastered and becomes habitual, it moves to the unconscious mind (fig. 5.1). By then, knowledge in the form of a skill has become habitual, and you are free to work on learning something else with the conscious mind.

It is, indeed, unfortunate when a rider learns a skill the wrong way, because as you will see later, what you learn first is easiest to remember and hardest to undo. If you learn the wrong way, you have to haul it back into the conscious brain, and it takes many conscious repetitions (some say 5,000) to delete the poor habit. Then it takes many more repetitions (some say 10,000!) to make the new habit automatic so it can go back to the unconscious brain. It's not a simple process.

Experienced teachers are aware of this phenomenon, so they don't mind repeating themselves. They are patient because they understand why a student doesn't catch on immediately and they understand the necessity of these repetitions. They also know how to reduce the number of repetitions required. Here, for example, are a few techniques you can try to reduce the number of repetitions needed:

- Mental practice can be as effective as physical practice. That is, riding in your mind is as valuable as actually riding. That's been proven by educational studies so when you practice in your mind, try to imagine your ride without any mistakes. Perfection isn't easy in real life, but in your mind you have the added benefit of being able to practice perfectly. When you practice riding

{5.1} The conscious mind is where learning takes place. When a skill is mastered and a habit established, it can be relegated to the unconscious mind. Then the conscious mind is free to work on the next learning challenge.

well in your mind, you will ride better in reality. Of course, if you mentally practice making mistakes, your fear of failure has won the race over your expectation of success, so empower yourself to ride like a champion in your mind!

- Associate a desirable habit with something pleasurable. For example, if you'd like to develop the habit of carrying your hands with your thumbs up, imagine holding an ice cream cone upright so it doesn't drip, or a glass of your favorite wine. You'll be inclined to hold those thumbs up to avoid spilling.

- Utilize The Principles of Learning that are outlined in Part Three (see p. 144). These principles explain many more ways of improving your speed of learning and your retention.

How Two Minds Meet:
The Mental Dynamics
of Dressage

Learning as an Amateur

Amateurs can be as good or better than professionals, if they work—and play—at it. What unique qualities does the amateur have? And what can amateurs do to maximize their progress?

- Amateurs often sit at an inanimate desk for eight hours before riding. So, when they get on the horse, they need and want to be in a different world. The horse provides this, but the rider needs to get physically up to speed. A little warm-up before getting on helps. The rider also needs to get mentally in a non-thinking mode. A brief, quiet meditation will sometimes help. Calm the mind and activate the body.

- They sometimes don't empower themselves to be as good as they can be because they simply think of themselves as amateurs. Forget that.

- Amateurs who work don't usually have great riders to watch and emulate because they often ride at night when everyone else has gone home or sometimes there isn't a great rider in their riding community to watch. An amateur student in Connecticut, Jessica Morgan, worked for an insurance company in Hartford. She rode her own horse a maximum of five days a week after long workdays at her job. When she finally could ride, it was usually dark, and although she had an indoor arena, the weather in Connecticut was often cold and icy, and everyone else had gone home. Then one year, she and her horse won the United States Dressage Federation (USDF) National Championship, placing first in the nation

WHAT TO DO
– Look Up –

AT the beginning of your ride, go around the entire riding area in walk without looking down once. If you look down, you have to start over. Afterward, go the other way without looking down once. Then you'll be inclined to keep that balance rather than starting out wrong and needing to make it right. Olympian and founder of Dressage4Kids Lendon Gray once commented to a group of largely amateur riders touring professional barns in Wellington, Florida, "Did you notice that all the riders we've watched are looking up? You don't need an expensive instructor to teach you to look up! You can do that for yourself!" ●

at Second Level for amateur owners. Perhaps even more impressive, they were second in the nation—USDF Reserve Champions by a fraction of a point—in the Open Division against all the professionals. How did she do it? Probably because she had developed the habit of watching the best riders in the world online. She did that long before it was popular. She often came to the barn saying, "Did you see Ingrid Klimke's latest ride?" Or, Did you see the winning ride at Dortmund (Germany) this weekend?" The power of imitation is tremendous, and the images in Jessie's mind were the best riders in the world. Anyone can watch those riders online, and it's usually free! Try it. (I'll talk more about imitation on p. 132.)

- Mental expectations are hard to change. If you're used to getting a canter depart that's obedient but not "through," it takes a degree of persistence and time to change that expectation to a different result. Sometimes you need to consciously set realistic goals and achieve them, bit by bit. Try to consciously revamp your expectations. Expect your horse to dance (for more, see Goal Setting—p. 183).

- Amateurs sometimes look down and round their shoulders when they ride because some of them spend too much time focusing on a computer screen. Amateurs and professionals alike often look down out of habit or sometimes because their seat and leg aren't balanced under them and they unknowingly use the head as a counterbalance.

- Amateurs who haven't been into the rhythm of riding and watching horses all day, often give aids

> **" Although the logical, thinking, knowledge-accumulating left brain is only a part of the rider's mental capacity, it's an important part because it informs and influences the other dimensions of the mind. "**

that are too slow. (Sometimes they're too fast or hectic, but they're usually too slow.) Learn the tempo of your horse's gaits by using a metronome, or an app on your phone can be a metronome for you. The walk is usually about 100 beats per minute. The trot varies between 140 to 160 beats per minute, and the canter is about 96 beats per minute. If you ride a pony, the tempos might be a little quicker. When you ride, be sure your aids are in the rhythm and tempo of your horse's gaits. As the leader, you need to be a metronome for your horse to help him keep the rhythm and tempo.

- Some amateurs have high-level management jobs and may have CEO-itis. They're used to delegating, "This needs doing. Please, do it. Fix this so it works, and then return it to me. Thank you." These people delegate jobs to others on the team who accomplish the task at hand. This is a perfectly appropriate way to operate in business, but it doesn't translate perfectly into the

The Plug for Knowledge

Some riders are focused too much on competition—getting the right horse and achievement. There's nothing wrong with this, but in the process, book learning sometimes suffers—especially with the youth, and there's plenty wrong with that.

All serious riders should understand the Training Scale so thoroughly they could easily give a 45-minute lecture on the subject. They should understand the concepts behind each quality in the Training Scale, and they should know the purposes of each level of dressage tests (see Appendix, p. 206). Many riders actually ride the tests without knowing the purpose—without knowing what they are supposed to prove! No one would ever do that in the classroom!

The Appendix that begins on page 196 is intended to touch upon some of the most important categories of equine knowledge. However, it does not touch upon the most important categories of horsemanship: riders should know about equine health, nutrition, special care in different climates, and the effects of different bits, to name just a few topics. There are worlds of information about horsemanship that go way beyond riding. At the end of the day, that underlying knowledge is what guides the training of every horse. When it comes to those riders standing up on the international podium, they have the knowledge. May there never be a day when the riders on the podium don't have that knowledge. Knowledge guides actions and determines results. That knowledge is accumulated and organized in the rider's "thinking" mind (see p. 78), and should lead to wise actions and strong, positive results! ●

world of horses. The professional trainer often *does* fix the horse so he works as well as possible and returns him to the owner, but ultimately it's up to each individual rider to work it out with her own horse. The horse isn't a machine, a software system, or a protocol. Some degree of human discernment is required. Also no matter how well trained, the horse will follow his rider, and over time, go to the level of his rider. Horses keep us very honest.

- Amateurs seem more inclined than professionals to beat themselves up for making a mistake and in the process miss the opportunity to teach the horse something (see the fictional Michelle on p. 67).

- Amateurs are sometimes quite academic and read more than professionals. They may, in fact, understand the concepts behind riding in harmony rather well. They can academically apply principles of learning and principles of riding.

Amateurs are often smart people who work at jobs that require their thinking powers. That amateur rider might, from the saddle, think, *I'm trying!* The question then is whether or not that rider is trying mentally or physically? Horses need physical aids, and amateurs often, in the name of invisible aids, don't make themselves clear physically. All riders should use their aids as little as possible BUT as much as necessary so the horse understands.

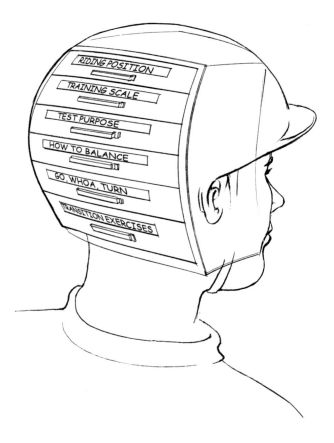

{5.2} Knowledge isn't very clear or useful until it is categorized.

84

How Two Minds Meet:
The Mental Dynamics
of Dressage

How Is Your Left Brain's Filing System?

Many riders have an enormous amount of knowledge, but that knowledge isn't very useful if it isn't categorized well. Information needs to be seen in the context of a larger picture. In fact, knowledge can be categorized in many different ways (fig. 5.2). For example, how would you categorize the important concept of *Rhythm*?

Here are a few ways:

- *Rhythm* is the bottom building block of the Training Scale otherwise known as the Pyramid of Training (see p. 151). It is the foundation upon which all horses are trained.

- The rhythm of your horse's gaits is his language and his method of expressing himself. Preservation and improvement of the horse's gaits means strict attention to rhythm.

- Clear rhythm is a key requirement in all the Training Level tests (as well as being a key requirement of all subsequent tests). The purpose of Training Level is: "To confirm that the horse demonstrates correct basics, is supple and moves freely forward in a clear *rhythm* with a steady tempo, accepting contact with the bit."

- Rhythm can be thought of in its relationship to the concept of tempo. The rhythm is the characteristic footfall of the gait: a four-beat walk, a two-beat trot, or a three-beat canter with a period of suspension. The tempo is the speed of that rhythm as measured by a metronome.

- Cadence is the accentuation or emphasizing of the rhythm as a result of added power or, in the case of riding horses, impulsion. When you think of the emphasis that impulsion brings to the rhythm, you may have an "Aha!" moment. You thought you knew all about rhythm, but now your understanding of it has been enhanced in light of your understanding of impulsion and cadence.

This could go on and on. Expansion of your system of categorizing knowledge not only helps your knowledge grow, but it also clarifies it, and your thoughts become uncluttered. As you know, horses don't understand clutter; they understand clarity. You can improve your brain's filing system and the clarity of your thoughts by categorizing them.

Examples of two categories of knowledge about training horses can be found in the Appendix:

- The Training Scale (the Pyramid of Training) is the recipe for training all horses.

- The Purposes of the USEF Dressage Tests provides guidelines for training horses through the levels.

There are many other categories of organized knowledge including:

- The three methods of balancing your horse: half-halts, transitions, and shoulder-fore (see p. 32).

- The principles of a correct riding position that balance you—a prerequisite for balancing your horse (I discuss these—as well as the points that follow—in detail in my first book *When Two Spines Align: Dressage Dynamics*).

- The three essential riding skills: go, whoa, and turn.

A List Can Help Your Brain

Years ago, German Olympian Isabell Werth was featured in a USDF Symposium. Her teaching was extraordinarily clear, simple, and persistent. The results of the riders under her tutelage were astounding. I left with new insights, and was determined to implement all of them and never forget! So I carried a list of her principles in my pocket when I rode. That list was made up of a refinement of ideas that I already knew, but Isabell's version of the concepts had not yet made it to my unconscious brain. When a behavior finally makes it to the unconscious brain, it is a habit you don't have to think about. The fact is that you can only think about and concentrate on one thing at a time, so having a list that you can check on during breaks reminds you of the things you need to work on consciously. A few of the items on my Isabell Werth list went like this:

- *Inside leg to outside rein.* (Of course, I already knew this, but Isabell's version of inside leg to outside rein was much more persistent and effective than I had been.)

- *Close the leg and push the horse's nose out.* I already knew this, too, but this was Isabell's version again. You had to do it until the horse honestly sought the bit and used his back like physical poetry.

- *When the horse flexes right or left correctly and yields to the bit, he is saying, "Yes!"* He becomes more supple and rideable because you are able to use the inside leg to the outside rein. That flexion determines which direction is "inside." Again and again, she said, "The horse must say, Yes!" Isabell's version of flexion was much clearer than mine had been and it was more persistent but never overflexed.

The list was on a 3 by 5 card, and it eventually became very ragged and difficult to read. By then, the concepts were deeply ingrained in my thinking, but it was hard to throw the list away because it had become more than the sum of its suggestions. It had come to represent clarity, lack of compromise, kindness, persistence, beauty, fun. It was quite a special list. I'll never forget it. ●

- Transition exercises that develop an ideal connection between horse and rider.

- Transition exercises that improve collection in the horse.

There are many more categories of knowledge and many layers of meaning behind each of the categories I've mentioned here, but it helps to keep a list in your mind so the enormous content behind each item is filed in the right place. There are certainly other checklists within your own mental filing system that may not be mentioned here but may be useful to you. However, training gets really interesting when you venture beyond the "thinking" mind. Great horsemen use their minds in a "non-thinking" way, too. They ride with two minds.

Essential Information About the Rider's Left Brain

✓ In most aspects of life, people are judged by how well they think, learn, and solve problems. This left-brained knowledge is important to riders. Understanding the many aspects of good horsemanship as well as the theory behind riding skills serves them well.

✓ The conscious mind can only concentrate on and learn one thing at a time. As soon as that skill is mastered and becomes habitual, it moves to the unconscious mind, and the learner is free to work on learning something else with the conscious mind.

✓ It is important to learn the right way first because it's difficult to unlearn.

✓ Riders do well to be able to categorize and organize their knowledge and then act on it.

SUMMARY 5

> THE "NON-THINKING" MIND IS IN THE MOMENT, AND IT CAN GO WITHIN, IN WHICH CASE WE CALL IT MEDITATION, OR IT CAN REACH OUTWARD WHERE IT IS RECEPTIVE TO THE UNIVERSE.

The Rider's Right Brain: Non-Thinking and Dynamic Meditation

6
CHAPTER

As you know, most people identify excessively with thinking, so it's easy to forget that there is another way to *be* other than by thinking. The "non-thinking" mind is in the moment, and it can go *within*, in which case we call it meditation, or it can reach *outward* where it is receptive to the universe. When it reaches out, it is often called prayer. It is communing with God or Nature or with other living beings—such as your horse.

In our everyday lives, most people don't use the other dimensions of the mind much. But as we know, our horses actually require that we explore those other dimensions. We need to go to the place where the horse is—that place where there is no wrangling with daily problems. Remember that horses don't understand negativity, they can't pass judgment, and they live totally in the present moment? When you can go to that place, you will be in a frame of mind that the horse can read.

The best riders ride with two minds: one that the horse cannot read and one that the horse can read. The rider's logical thinking, learning, knowledge-accumulating, problem-solving mind that is so important to us is the mind that the horse *cannot* read. The "non-thinking" mind is the one that your horse *can* read. It's also the mind that feels and listens to the horse and makes for two-way constructive conversation. During your ride, you can switch back and forth between thinking and non-thinking. The thinking mind that your horse can't read, guides *you* well, but your non-thinking mind guides *him* well.

*The best riders ride
with two minds: one that
the horse cannot read and
one that the horse can read.*

Here's an example: you would like to perfect your horse's canter depart, so your deliberate thinking mind has planned an exercise to help him (fig. 6.1):

- You plan to turn down the quarterline in trot.

- You will ride a shallow leg-yield to the track. This leg-yield should improve your connection and succeed in getting your horse's hind legs in a good position to do the canter depart.

- When you get to the rail, you'll ask for a canter depart.

This planning was the deliberate *thinking* behind the exercise. And there's more thinking:

- It helps to know where your horse's legs are and to understand the diagonal nature of the trot, which is your gait of choice for this leg-yield.

- You need to understand the specific line of travel and be mentally committed to it. If he falls off this line of travel, he'll lose his balance.

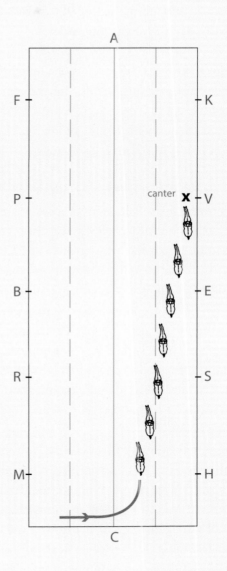

{6.1} Exercise for the Left Brain's Plan for the Canter Depart

- You need to know other technical aspects of the exercise: flexion away from the line of travel determines which are the *inside* and the *outside* of the horse. You'll want to ride from inside leg to outside rein along the line of travel and keep his body parallel to the long side.

- It helps to know the dynamics of a half-halt and where your horse's legs are during each part of it.

- You need to know the timing of the hind leg that will strike off into the canter depart.

- You need to have information about your horse and how he feels. Is he nervous? Is he comfortable? Does he know what's coming? Will he anticipate in a good way or does anticipation make him anxious? If the latter, maybe you'll take a tiny walk break each time you finish an exercise. There are thousands of variables in that department.

All this information needs to have spilled from your conscious mind to your unconscious mind so you can have instant access to it and be free to *feel* your horse.

The actual riding of this exercise is about feeling and sensation. It's about non-thinking and being, as you know, in the dynamic meditation of the *now* with your horse, which some have called a state of pure sensation or being "in the Zone."

You are swinging in the two beats of trot, feeling the weight bearing moment, and feeling how the thrust inflates his forehand as the shoulder reaches with the possibility of a new degree of freedom. You feel (but don't think about) the right moment to ask for the canter depart. You soften invisibly into the new gait, and so on.

After the exercise, you probably slip back to your thoughts and get judgmental about your horse's degree of success. *Should you repeat the exercise? Is he getting tired and perhaps it would be smart to take a break?* Now you have access to your thoughts again. Skilled riders have easy access to these thoughts when they're in the Zone. They don't need to "think" about them because they have learned them so well that they are in the unconscious.

The non-thinking mind senses. It has no opinion, it is automatic, and is in the *now*—in the Zone (fig. 6.2). When you're in the Zone, you're in your "right" mind for riding. Sally Swift, author of *Centered Riding*, called it "soft eyes." You're physically and mentally focused, attentive, absorbed, and you enter a state—a Zone—in which your performance often excels inexplicably.

● Finding the Zone

What *is* this non-thinking dynamic meditation with infinite capacity? How did Sue Blinks (see fig. 6.2) get to that place? How do *we* get to that place? We need to find a reliable way to find that quiet place within—to find those other dimensions of the mind that are void of thought but have infinite capacity (fig. 6.3). It is the beautiful, simple place of dynamic meditation where magic sneaks in the door and opens your world to infinite possibilities.

It's often difficult to find the Zone because the thinking mind is capable of going rogue—and it often does. When the thinking mind goes rogue,

{6.2} Sue Blinks is "in the Zone" here as she rides Flim Flam for the United States in the 2000 Sydney Olympic Games.

{6.3} The non-thinking mind has infinite capacity. The performance of athletes in the Zone sometimes excels inexplicably.

it's the makings of insomnia by night and inefficiency by day. Compulsive thinking is the mindless internal, often negative chatter sometimes called "monkey mind" (see fig. 7.1, p. 102). We sometimes can't get out of the thinking mind; we can't stop the list-making, the mathematical figuring, the analyzing, the weighing of options. All of us have times when we're frazzled, and it's hard to stop thinking. A song that you dislike keeps going through your head. *It's a Small World….* That's compulsive. Monkey mind limits our possibilities and transforms the quality of our entire lives from the spiritual realm to the mundane.

In the space between monkey mind and the Zone is "deliberate thinking." That's a step in the right direction. And a step beyond that (and how do you take this next step?) is the ability to stop thinking and go to that quiet, meditative, non-thinking place that is simpler than thought, but at the same time, far beyond thought. That Zone is where the magic begins. What gets in the way? Often, it is emotion.

How Two Minds Meet:
The Mental Dynamics
of Dressage

The non-thinking mind senses.
It has no opinion,
it is automatic, and is
*in the **now**—in the Zone.*

● **Seeking Positive Emotion**

Emotion in both horse and rider—and in life—can be friend or foe. Emotion is the underlying attitude with which we couch the things we think and do. It is either the delicious sauce that enhances our thoughts and actions, or it is the poison that minimizes our chances for success by tainting our thoughts and actions.

Success in communicating with horses has a lot to do with the emotion in which every communication is couched. It's the same as conversations between people. It's not always *what* a colleague said at the meeting but *how* he said it. Likewise, *what* you say with your aids isn't necessarily negative or positive. How you *feel* about what you are saying—*and* how you feel as a result of external personal circumstances—will either be the delicious sauce or the poison, or more often, an emotion somewhere on the spectrum in between.

For example, when a rider gives her horse a little kick forward, she might be thinking, *Come on, you can do this!* Or, she might be thinking, *You stupid cow!* The horse knows the *feeling* and the *intention* behind that nudge forward. He knows.

Emotions can be roughly categorized into some form of either fear or love. Subcategories of love are hope, peace, appreciation, optimism, kindness, empathy, gratitude, respect, curiosity, and joy. There are other positive emotions, too, and they all encourage physical relaxation and mental comfort.

Subcategories of fear are jealousy, sadness, envy, anger, hatred, pessimism, anxiety, and other negative emotions. These emotions inevitably manifest themselves in physical and mental tension, and they can trigger fight, flight or, in the case of humans, negotiation. Humans have the advanced ability to see one another's point of view, so they have the ability to negotiate.

Love and fear (along with their associated emotions) can't live comfortably in the same place at the same time. In other words, you can't feel anger and respect at the same time. Think about it. You can't feel jealousy and gratitude at the same time. They can't reside together.

You can't have pessimistic feelings, and also feel honest curiosity. Try it. It's not possible to have the feeling of *I wonder…* when, for example, you're feeling anxious about your ability to finish your project by a deadline. Riding horses is all about wonder, so your riding will suffer unless you can put those anxious feelings aside. Quiet communication between you and your horse only happens when you're able to stop the monkey mind.

The sympathetic nervous system, in both horse and rider, regulates fight and flight. Its activation kills the ability to be present. That's the case for both horse and rider, so when we're worried, or in a state of fear or an emotion related to fear,

Jealousy, Envy
Anger, Hatred
Pessimism
Anxiety

Peace, Kindness
Hope, Appreciation
Optimism, Kindness
Empathy, Gratitude

● {6.4} Love and fear cannot coexist. Love, along with other related positive emotions, encourages physical relaxation and mental comfort. Fear, along with other related negative emotions, inevitably manifests itself in physical and mental tension.

we can't be present, we can't listen or concentrate well, or learn. We can't be positive or compassionate. Nothing works well. In everyday life, this is why people who are ill need an advocate. When a person is impaired, for example, by some level of anxiety about his health, he can't also be a good listener. What did the doctor say during that appointment? It's rarely clear.

Negativity prevents one from being in the Zone, and unfortunately, the human brain is inclined to focus on the negative. Brenda Selgado, author of *Real World Mindfulness for Beginners* (Sonoma Press, 2016), calls this inclination "the negativity bias." She says, "Research shows that negative experiences are immediately stored in long-term memory, whereas it takes positive experiences 12 to 20 seconds to be stored in long-term memory." Feelings of fight or flight win.

Hans Rosling, in his book called *Factfulness* (Flatiron, 2020), called this human inclination

How Two Minds Meet: The Mental Dynamics of Dressage

"the negativity instinct"—the tendency to notice the bad more than the good. Awareness of this human tendency to favor negativity can prevent it from influencing our attitudes too strongly. You know how horses experience negativity. With confusion.

How do you get in the Zone—in that place where you are informed and influenced by logic and knowledge but empty of it? Imagine the Zone with little entrances everywhere that are easy to find if you know how to go about it. The entrances to the Zone are not locational, and the Zone isn't somewhere else. It's in you, and the keys to the entrances are behavioral—the same behaviors that you use to stop compulsive and even deliberate thinking.

All these behaviors require you to be mentally positive and present, to reach outward, be compassionate and curious, and finally to be receptive—listen and concentrate. Horses, in fact, require that we be on our best behavior.

But first let's look, in the next chapter, at the "dark side," just so we know how to avoid it or at least make the best of it.

s u m m a r y   o f   c h a p t e r   6

Essential Information About Non-Thinking and Dynamic Meditation

✓ The best riders ride with two minds: the logical, thinking, learning, knowledge-accumulating left brain and the non-thinking, dynamically meditative right brain. The horse can understand the latter.

✓ The "Zone" is that frame of mind in which performance often excels inexplicably, and athletes try to achieve that frame of mind.

✓ Negative emotions such as fear, criticism, anger, anxiety, self-absorption, and preoccupation with external situations prevent one from being in the Zone.

SUMMARY 6

"
EMOTIONAL POISONS
ARE A PART OF EVERYONE'S LIFE.
WE JUST NEED TO LEARN
HOW TO MANAGE THEM.

Managing Emotional Poisons

On the poison end of the spectrum of emotions, some riders are chronically crabby, preoccupied, self-centered, overly serious, or even angry, and a beautiful partnership can never evolve in these atmospheres.

Negative attitudes and distractions belong to real, wonderful people. Sometimes they are us. Sometimes they are riders who are highly valued in other aspects of their lives. The surgeon is out there saving lives on a daily basis. She can't leave her phone in the car when she comes to ride. So why does she ride? Probably so she can learn to put her daily challenges aside, but it must be difficult. The family attorney, an hour before getting on her horse, was dealing with the placement of a beautiful child with either a dysfunctional mother or an out-of-state father. The business executive was delegating his problems and having them fixed by someone else. That won't work for long with his or her horse. The attorney may be in fight mode. She was trained to counterattack and might have trouble getting out of that mode. The secretary has been crouched over a computer all day and has trouble sitting tall and looking up. The mom is wondering if she'll get home before the school bus drops off her six-year-old.

Wow. The horse is doing a tremendous service to all these people, but some of the riders aren't able to maximize their opportunities in the saddle because it just isn't easy to make a delicious sauce every single day. In fact, these distractions are, by most measures, more important than refining the shoulder-in. Regardless, the horse doesn't know these aspects of his rider's life and will consistently disappoint the rider who

*The horse's persistent lesson is to help the rider come to the saddle every day as a blank slate and experience the **now**.*

is "chronically crabby, self-centered, overly serious or preoccupied."

The horse's persistent lesson is to help the rider come to the table (or the saddle) every day as a blank slate and experience the *now*. The horse teaches you to retain or regain your sense of self in the face of personal challenges. Riding is good therapy because the horse mirrors our strengths and our weaknesses. When you bring tension to the saddle, you'll get tension. Unfortunately, when you bring relaxation to the saddle, you won't necessarily get relaxation. That's not fair, is it? Life isn't fair. Riding tells us a lot about ourselves. With amazing accuracy, horses even have physical problems in the same places as their riders.

● Starving the Evil Wolf

Fear comes in lots of colors and sizes. Fear of failure, fear of getting hurt physically, and even fear of success. Fear of hurting the horse in rehab, fear of losing the ride, fear of losing your job. It can come in the form of being timid, anxious, or downright afraid.

Whether you are the teacher of a timid student or you *are* the timid student, ask, "Is there

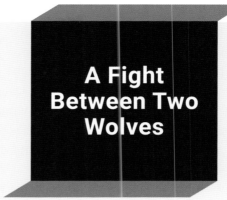

A Fight Between Two Wolves

AN old Cherokee was teaching his grandson about life. "A fight is going on inside me," he said to the boy. "It is a terrible fight and it is between two wolves. One is evil—he is anger, envy, sorrow, regret, greed, arrogance, self-pity, guilt, resentment, inferiority, lies, false pride, superiority, and ego."

He paused, then continued, "The other is good—he is joy, peace, love, hope, serenity, humility, kindness, benevolence, empathy, generosity, truth, compassion, and faith.

"The same fight is going on inside you—and inside every other person, too."

The grandson thought about it for a minute and asked his grandfather, "Which wolf will win?"

The old man simply replied, "The one you feed." ●

a good reason for this timidity?" Feelings of fear are sometimes well-founded and riders would do well to pay attention to their fears. Maybe you should ride a different horse either because the horse is ill-tempered or because he is inappropriate for any number of reasons. Much has been written about how to gain your horse's trust, but your horse also has to be trustworthy!

Anger is another emotional poison. Riders never revert to anger when they know what they're

Horses primarily experience ***now***, *so to communicate with them successfully, you need to be in the* ***now*** *also.*

doing. Eventing superstar Denny Emerson said, "Anger begins where knowledge leaves off." The best advice for the angry rider is to get off.

The judgmental critic is another negative, and there's no place for him while you're riding. As soon as you find this armchair critic sitting on your shoulder and empowering your monkey mind, find a way to shake him off (fig. 7.1). But when the critic is real and sitting on a bench in the corner of the arena, that's another story (see Social Learning on p. 144).

The critic can be positive, of course. Most riders try constantly to make positive changes to their riding position or to their training plan. They wonder if they could be doing something better, and they welcome guidance and feedback from knowledgeable trainers and other good riders. These changes just need to be made in a positive way. Remember the list you carry in your pocket? Those left-brained critiques can be acknowledged and addressed in a positive way.

Negative tension is tight and physically not supple. The rider who has negative tension can't be harmonious or grounded. Physical tension is also a reflection of mental tension and a lack of open mindedness.

● {7.1} There's no critic quite as tough as the monkey mind of the self. Find a way to shake off self-criticism and replace it with constructive self-talk.

How Two Minds Meet: The Mental Dynamics of Dressage

Complaining is the opposite of gratitude. Just as gratitude invites more good stuff into your life, complaining focuses on the aspects of life that you don't want and strengthens those things. What you pay attention to grows.

Scattered or disorganized thinking is common among people who are feeding the evil wolf. Of course they don't know they are doing this, but without a clear plan, their efforts are like stabs in the dark, and, of course, horses don't understand scattered and disorganized thinking.

But, as you know, the negative bias or the negative instinct is a human condition, and it affects all of us. The best we can do is be aware of and manage it.

● Managing the Negative

Task-Oriented Riding

Instructors can often dispel the negative by making the lesson *task-oriented.* The focus becomes how well the horse did the exercise instead of how well the rider is controlling the horse. In the process, of course, doing any exercise builds up the rider as the leader and the horse as the follower, so it helps the rider gain control.

For the rider who often rides without instruction, the task-oriented system will help keep both horse and rider focused "on task."

> ★ **Try This**

Exercise for Task-Oriented Riding

1. Track left and go down the centerline (fig. 7.2).

● {7.2} Exercise for Task-Oriented Riding

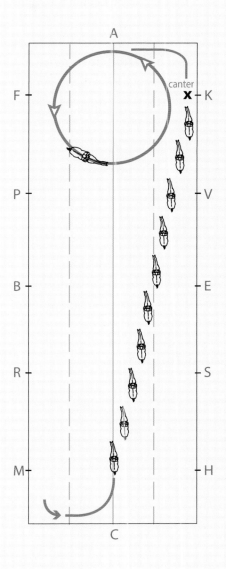

103

2. Leg-yield right to the corner letter. Do the task in both directions one or two times and take a break.

3. Next do the same task with an added challenge: After leg-yielding to the corner letter, develop canter and at the center of the short side, circle 15 meters.

4. Change across the diagonal. Trot at X and repeat in the other direction. Take another break and do another task.

This is task-oriented riding, and it puts the rider in a good position. Even if the task isn't well done, the focus doesn't spiral into a situation in which the tail is wagging the dog. The rider is calling the shots, and the performance of each task will improve with repetition. Make up exercises like this one that are appropriate for your own horse.

Emotional Toughness

Emotional toughness is being fearless in the face of disappointment or challenges and being open to new things. It is being sponge-like and hungry for knowledge. The emotionally tough rider doesn't mind being humbled because that's how she learns new things. Every time she is put down a peg, she is actually learning a new aspect of training horses. So what seems like going *down* a peg is actually going *up* a peg. The emotionally tough rider sees that failure as evidence of growth. She finds a kernel of pleasure in failure because she learns from it.

Mirrors, videos cameras, and eyes on the ground can be tough on the ego, but it's the only way to go. Years ago, a trainer taught two cheerful women who took lessons at the same time each week for years. One day the trainer decided to video her faithful students. She forwarded the footage as they pulled out of the driveway and never saw them again! The truth can be painful, but it's your first line of offense.

The emotionally tough rider welcomes learning experiences. She doesn't mind, for example, being put on a longe line to help perfect her position on a large circle. The ideal rider welcomes these apparent little steps down. This doesn't mean she doesn't feel disappointed with lower-than-normal scores, but she searches for the judge's comments and welcomes the opportunity to learn so she can improve the next time. There is no obsession over the need to "arrive." The mentally tough rider enjoys the journey.

Fight, Flight—or Negotiate

The "fight-or-flight" instinct isn't only for horses. People at war either stand their ground and fight or they retreat. But, because people are more evolved than other animals, they have a third option—one that's positive. They have the ability to negotiate and be diplomatic. They try to see each other's point of view, which is the quality that can make us good horse trainers.

There *is* a conflict of interest inherent in the horse-and-rider relationship: the rider wants and needs control while her horse wants to retain his innate spirit and sense of freedom. (This conflict can get worked out and was described in detail in *When Two Spines Align*.)

Control the Controllables

German trainer Conrad Schumacher said, "Control the controllables," and he meant that you shouldn't be mentally distracted about things you can't control. You can't do anything about the weather, but you can decide if you're going to ride in footing that might be compromised by the weather. You can't do anything about the time constriction within which you must ride, but you can do something about how you use your time.

You can vow not to ride with a hurried attitude. The Zone is out of reach when you're being chased by the clock.

Know what you can and cannot influence, and make wise decisions.

It seems that we rarely see riding couched in negativity nowadays—probably because it doesn't work. Horses train us to feed the good wolf and be our best selves. The bottom line is that emotional poisons are a part of everyone's life. We just need to learn how to manage them.

Essential Information About Emotional Poisons

✓ Emotional poisons are a normal part of everyone's life.

✓ We all need to learn how to "starve the evil wolf" by managing the emotional poisons in our lives.

✓ In addition to fight-and-flight instincts, humans have the ability to negotiate because they can see another point of view—in this case, the horse's point of view.

✓ Task-oriented riding can put you in the position of leader and help you ride with clarity.

✓ Learning to be emotionally tough can help you become mentally open to learning and progressing.

✓ When you control the controllables, you don't waste energy worrying about aspects of life that you *can't* control.

SUMMARY 7

105

THE HORSE REQUIRES YOU TO REACH OUT IN A SPIRIT OF RECEPTIVITY. LISTEN TO HIM, AND FEEL CURIOSITY AND WONDER.

Positive Behaviors and the Zone

8

CHAPTER

ccess to the Zone (see chapter 6, p. 89) starts with tossing your ego out the door. The horse doesn't care if you're a famous novelist or the CEO of a Fortune 500 company. He doesn't care if your father is a rock star or a famous football player. He also doesn't care if you have no claim to fame. He doesn't think less of you for it.

It's the same with any sport. The basketball, the baseball, the golf ball—they don't care. You get no break for your credentials and no disrespect for your lack of credentials. That's the beautiful nature of all sport. But the horse, unlike those balls, is blood and bone, heart and soul.

The horse takes you even farther down the evolutionary road, by requiring you reach out to him in a spirit of receptivity—that you listen and feel compassion, empathy, kindness, benevolence, humility, and gratitude. He requires you acknowledge the truth for what it is without sugar-coating it or embellishing it with positive or negative drama. The horse requires that you to have faith in that truth and in the processes of life—of health and growth—and that you have faith in the time-honored process of training horses that we call by its French word, "dressage."

The source for all this goodness is an underlying love for the horse, and the result of meeting all of the horse's quiet requests is an underlying feeling of peace, serenity, and joy. In short, the horse requires that we be our very best selves. This is serious fuel for the magic that occurs in the Zone, and it's fuel for the charming addiction that befalls so many horsemen.

*Riding horses
is all about wonder,
and wonder is the basis
of all good conversation.*

It all clearly takes place in the part of the mind that is *non-thinking*, and it involves reaching outward in an egoless and receptive state.

● How to Listen

Do you know anyone who is truly a good listener? Someone who looks you in the eye and hears what you have to say without mentally rehearsing her response? Someone who doesn't have a preconceived notion that she is right—and perhaps that you are wrong? She who is truly a good listener is, of course, truly informed, and when she does finally have something to say, everyone listens to her. It's the same when conversing with horses.

A good listener is curious, searching for the truth whether it be in politics and world affairs or within the tiny world of rider and horse. Curiosity is a questioning state of mind—the ability to reach out and say, *I wonder.* Riding horses is all about wonder. *I wonder. I wonder how you feel today? I wonder if you can step under my seat? I wonder if you can go promptly? Can you stop without me using my hands?*

Wonder. Because you wonder, you ask your horse questions and receive answers. Wonder is the basis of all good conversation. The state of being wonder-FUL holds the promise of many conversations that require *listening* skills. In order to listen, the mental traffic that is typically headed in a direction that is ironically called "out of your mind," is forced to do a U-turn and head in the other direction to allow traffic to go "into your mind." When you're listening, the mental traffic is entering your mind. In normal conversation, the traffic goes both ways—in and out.

With your physical aids, as you know, you alternate between active and passive aids. It's the same with the mind. You can be active but also passive. There is a physical circle of energy when riding horses (which I detail in *When Two Spines Align*), and I imagine that there is a comparable mental circle of energy (fig. 8.1). Traffic flows in and flows out in balance.

We're accustomed to "listening" being the purview of our ears, but as most people know, we can listen with other senses to increase awareness and feeling. For example, pay attention to your sense of smell. When the aroma of cinnamon buns is wafting through your kitchen, "monkey mind" disappears. When you notice the scent of a lilac bush, you can't be, at the same time, figuring something out or criticizing it. Just try.

Become aware of your sense of hearing. Listen to a great vocalist singing…there's not much thinking going on during that.

Use your sight. Look at a brilliant work of art or the natural beauty of the ocean, and analytical thought disappears.

A delectable feast will trigger the salivary response, and the perfect wine coupling isn't a taste that can be described with words, so most of us don't even try.

109

And, then there's the sense of touch—the sense that all riders seek to master. The sound and the tempo and the feel of that swinging trot is so sensually engrossing that thinking is impossible although access to the knowledge we've learned is available at will—as a kind of backdrop that is always there. It must be similar to how horses experience information. Once they are cultured about a concept or movement, they don't think about it. It just is.

Occasionally, we see riders who talk and talk and talk while they're riding, which, after a point,

The horse requires that you acknowledge the truth for what it is without sugar-coating it or embellishing it with positive or negative drama.

is just plain disrespectful to the horse. Olympian Sue Blinks says, "It's a waste of your horse's time." Quality riding requires listening to your horse—even when you're taking a break. Silence is more important than you might think. Research shows that brain cells actually regenerate during silence.

● Feeding the Good Wolf

Love and compassion require reaching outward—reaching beyond the ego toward another living being. They involve care, concern, sympathy, kindness, and other positive emotions that are directed outward—away from the self. Because compassion is directed outward, it's never self-absorbed, so it involves a complete lack of ego. Compassion also immerses us in the *now*. Compassion is current. It's about what you feel now rather than how you felt yesterday or how you will feel tomorrow.

Most riders and horsemen in associated careers innately love horses, so they are way ahead of the game. This underlying joy is fuel for the magic. Love surrounds and cushions every action the horseman makes. When the rider disciplines the horse firmly,

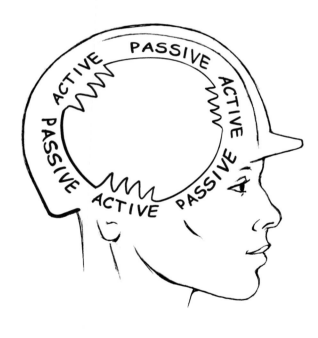

● {8.1} Most gifted conversationalists are good listeners. They listen and then they speak and listen again. The mental traffic goes in and out in balance. It's the same with riders. Riders need to be good listeners and clear "speakers."

110

How Two Minds Meet: The Mental Dynamics of Dressage

that love is still there, and it makes a difference. When love for the horse is the omnipresent underlying emotion in riding, it transcends all mistakes, misunderstandings, and even transgressions.

Love for the horse influences everything. The key word is "underlying" because at any given moment, a horse might be difficult in several of a thousand different ways, but when the rider's basic emotion is positive, the whole experience is essentially positive. For example, you may be riding a horse who is heavy on the left rein, spooking at a ghost in the bushes, or distracted by a spotted pony on the horizon, but your basic emotion can still be essentially compassionate.

Positive thoughts always precede positive action. As you know, we're successful with horses when we communicate what we want. We fail when we focus on what we don't want. Horses give humans this extraordinary gift of positive thinking because they don't understand the negative.

Mindfulness

Mindfulness is the active attention to the *now*, so being mindful is a prerequisite when communicating with your horse. The mindful rider is thoughtful because she pays attention to all the little details that make up a given situation.

In her book, *Real World Mindfulness for Beginners* (Sonoma Press, 2016), Brenda Salgado speaks of the "basic skills for mindfulness." These points all sound familiar to equestrians. These same principles help us enter the Zone where we can communicate with our horses and ride effectively:

- **Noticing the present moment.** *As you concentrate on the present moment, you are able to listen deeply to your horse.*

- **Staying grounded and in your body.** *Positive tension grounded to the earth is what makes riders strong. It's tempting, in the face of difficulties, to lift yourself, thereby losing the body's innate organization and grounded state. Grounded, positive tension is the easy way to be strong (see p. 68).*

- **Recognizing thoughts and emotions for what they are.** *Thoughts and emotions inform positively, but we should realize they don't represent the whole truth. We acknowledge shortcomings and work on them.*

- **Encouraging curiosity and a nonjudgmental attitude.** *Curiosity and a nonjudgmental attitude are what you need to bring to the saddle as a rider. You need to put the inner critic aside and open yourself up to learning from your horse by listening to him.* ●

{8.2} Grounded positive tension utilizes the entire body and is extremely strong. Not only that, athletes with positive mental tension have a keen, positive outlook along with increased awareness and mental acuity. This young athlete has found the Zone.

Positive tension is physically "stretchy" and strong rather than contracted and strong (fig. 8.2). This quality of positive tension is about physical and mental "reach." The horse reaches toward the bit. He reaches with his hind legs and shoulders. The rider reaches down and grounds herself to the earth, she reaches up through her spine to the crown of her head toward the sky. She reaches from her center, through her elbow toward the bit. She reaches to excel.

I explored this quality of positive tension in chapter 2 of *When Two Spines Align*: "When your body is open, your muscles are stretched,

How Two Minds Meet:
The Mental Dynamics
of Dressage

and you're in a state of positive tension—that is, *tension with suppleness.* In contrast, when your body is closed, the muscles are tightly clenched and you're in a state of negative tension. Lack of tension or slack relaxation also has the effect of closing the body."

Positive tension, when it is grounded to the earth, is extremely strong, and it is the easy way to be strong. Believe it or not, positive tension is not only reflected in your posture, but also in your emotion. It is open, receptive, and joyous. Horses and riders with positive mental tension have a keen, positive outlook along with increased awareness and mental acuity. Not only that, but positive mental tension brings with it a sense of self-fulfillment. Just as grounded positive tension in the body utilizes the entire body, positive tension is emotionally fulfilling (fig. 8.3).

Playfulness is the "right" mind for riding, which is more about feeling than thinking. It's not overly serious. The playful mentality enables creative solutions to common problems. Riding should be fun for both horse and rider. Challenge yourself and your horse in a way that your horse will have fun! Does he think you're fun? Does he try to please you? If not, why not? Are you letting him know when you're pleased? Don't underestimate the value of gratitude.

An *"attitude of gratitude"* gets rewarded. The universe somehow delivers to people who express gratitude. It always pays off, from a universal perspective as well as a relational one. The rider who innately feels the need to express her thanks when the horse performs well will bond with the horse and develop an obedient, happy partner. The rewards of gratitude are far flung.

Thoughtfulness

One of the greatest compliments you can give a rider is to say that she's "thoughtful." The thoughtful rider is caring, listens to her horse, and honors his nature as she works with him. But imagine this rider's mental state during the actual moments in which she's caring, listening, and honoring his nature. Is she thinking? No. Thinking has subsided. She's in the Zone, in the *now,* the state of non-thinking dynamic meditation that is the opposite of thinking.

So why do we call that "thoughtful?" The rider is not "full of thoughts," so maybe the word is just a misnomer. It's still a nice word. ●

113

Patience comes from having faith in the process and having a big toolbox of training skills. Dressage riders tend to be process-oriented rather than outcome-oriented. For example, *process-oriented* riders don't mind going back to the basics and regaining the prerequisites that will make a movement easy for the horse. For example, when the leg-yield starts to get crooked, the process-oriented rider will simply straighten her horse and try again. When the second four-tempi change is crooked, she won't consider asking for the third one. The *outcome-oriented* rider feels compelled to crank them out.

Making an outcome-oriented rider into a process-oriented rider is like changing her religion. It's not easy, but the process has been proven to deliver the outcome!

Process-oriented riders also don't expect the horse to give them an emotional "high" every day. Experienced horsemen don't let a "bad ride" ruin their day. They expect the normal range of human experience to be comparable to the normal range of experience with their horse. They are pleased with a small amount of progress because they know the horse can absorb only so much in a session.

When you fully understand how transitions develop the connection and then collection, you quietly and patiently do transitions until you get the connection you want. Then, and only then, do you work on collection. The system always, always works with horses who are sound because the system is based on the laws of nature. The process takes time, but it produces happy horses who maximize their potential. When you're process-oriented, you're inclined to have patience—but, ideally, not too much patience. Dressage takes time, but you don't want to waste time, either.

> "
> *Quality riding requires listening to your horse—even when you're taking a break. Silence is more important than you might think.*
> "

Persistent consistency (which I talked about on p. 60) is a quality associated with self-perfection or at least improvement in the face of some difficulty. Olympian and renowned educator Kyra Kyrklund said that the difference between Olympians and the rest of the riders in the world is simply a matter of persistence regarding the basics. Kyra brings all the necessary ingredients to the table: love of the horse, attention to detail, and persistence about getting all these details right in a playful, often humorous way. More recently, Charlotte Dujardin echoed Kyrklund's feelings about persistence and said that every rider is able, for example, to do good transitions, but the best riders *always* ride good transitions. If they make a poor transition, they correct it by making a good one, so the horse, in the end, only knows how to do good transitions. It's that persistent concentration on the basics that makes good riders great.

● Mental Health and Riding

Because riding horses brings out our best selves, our sport has a positive influence on mental health

How Two Minds Meet:
The Mental Dynamics
of Dressage

{8.3} Debbie McDonald, at only 5 feet tall, was as effective on Brentina as she would have been if she were 6 feet tall, because when she is riding, she uses all she has—from the soles of her feet to the crown of her head. Positive tension throughout the entire body grounds her and makes her very strong. Positive tension creates feelings of mental and emotional fulfillment.

for the reasons we've already discussed. A relationship with horses encourages us to develop healthy attitudes and emotions while discouraging negativity. Also, whereas any physical exercise promotes mental health, exercising with another living being builds trust and faith. It organically requires that you converse in a balance of give and take within an atmosphere of kindness and gratitude.

However, subsidiary aspects of riding can be mentally and emotionally challenging. For example, training horses can be financially demanding because horses, with their dietary, veterinary, farrier and other needs are unreasonably expensive. Many riders aren't educated in business and finance. Professionals are not always prepared to deal with the mathematics of it, and they might be dismayed by the demands of sometimes unreasonable clients.

Uncertainty regarding the health and soundness of horses, at some point, becomes an issue for every equestrian. One can prepare for an important show for years, and then the horse injures himself before the big event. Even when horse and rider are able to ride down the centerline, winning doesn't happen all that often and can be hard on the ego as well as the pocketbook.

The lifestyle of equestrians is physically demanding too. As a form of farming, the successful rider faces days, weeks, months and years of hard work.

Finding balance between personal and horse lives can be challenging for amateurs and professionals alike. Some riders find help from meditation, and professionals might seek help from outside experts who are educated in the horse industry: an accountant, a sports psychologist,

> **Because riding horses brings out our best selves, our sport has a positive influence on mental health.**

a general psychologist, a physical therapist, a primary care physician and whoever else might fill a need. Peer support groups often take the form of professionals and amateurs gatherings at conventions and conferences where like-minded people gather to learn, enjoy their friends, and realize that they're not alone. These get-togethers help tremendously.

The bottom line is that the most challenging kind of stress is the kind that you can't influence or control, and many of a rider's challenges fall into that category.

How Two Minds Meet:
The Mental Dynamics
of Dressage

Essential Information About Positivity That Invites You into the Zone

✓ The horse requires you to reach out in a spirit of receptivity; listen to him; and feel curiosity and wonder.

✓ He requires you to acknowledge the truth for what it is and that you have faith in the time-honored process of training.

✓ The horse requires you to be your very best self and deal with him with love, compassion, positivity, and gratitude.

✓ Mindfulness, the state of being in the *now* and grounded in reality in an open, non-judgmental way, is the way for successful equestrians.

✓ These positive qualities are prerequisites to being in the "Zone" where you can communicate with the horse optimally.

✓ The many innately positive aspects of riding horses help develop mental health for riders, but the sport poses significant challenges because of the expense of horse care, the time required to train horses, and uncertainty regarding their health and soundness.

SUMMARY 8

YOU CAN FOLD YOUR INTENTIONS
INTO YOUR CONCENTRATION
TO IMPROVE ANY QUALITY
OF YOUR RIDING.

Awareness, Concentration, and Intention

9

What you pay attention to grows. You can change and make improvements to your ride when you pay attention—when you concentrate on it. Concentration begins with simple *awareness* of, for example, your precise line of travel or your horse's rhythm, and it ends with being in the Zone where you are clearly present.

When you're aware of your planned line of travel, you can concentrate on following it, and if you're aware of your horse's rhythm, you can swing with it. When you're aware of the floor of your seat and how your horse's back moves, you can concentrate on following it, and if you're aware of how your horse's neck and head move, you can concentrate on following it with your rein contact. Awareness of your breathing and your horse's breathing brings you to the place. The depth of your awareness affects the quality of your concentration.

Concentration while riding is a dynamic meditation. You are dynamically in the *now,* which as you know, is a moving target when you're riding, and there's no sense of time as we usually think of time— as time passing. There's no yesterday, no tomorrow, no thought. There is only the *now* when you're concentrating.

● Fold Your Intentions into Your Concentration

Your *intentions* may or may not get incorporated into whatever you're concentrating on. For example, if you do yoga with the intention and the expectation that you will become more supple and strong, then

*Lack of intention
brings little
or no transformation.*

that is likely to happen. Your intentions transform reality. If you were to do the exact same yoga program without any expectations, your improvement would be weaker or maybe you wouldn't improve at all. Lack of intention brings little or no transformation.

Is your intention known to your horse? If you're not sure, then your aids probably aren't clear enough. Some riders are so subtle that the horse has no idea what his rider wants. Other riders are too loud to be "heard." Where are your aids?

Be *consequent* (see p. 29). There must be a re-action to your physical aids that is specific to the task. As you train your horse, you might think of leg-yield only because you are required to do it in a test, and then at another time, you might do a leg-yield and concentrate on the reason why you are doing it—for example, to improve the connection from the inside leg to the outside rein. The results of this leg-yield with intention will typically be better.

If you understand lateral balance, you will automatically align your horse with shoulder-fore in the rhythm of the gait without thinking about

it. If you do shoulder-fore without that desired result in mind, you probably won't achieve that result—or you will achieve it by rote and feel the straightness. Then your horse will tell you, *Yes! This is it.*

If you understand longitudinal balance you will automatically do half-halts and transitions with whatever level of skill you have, and the balance will improve. Your intentions get folded into the rhythm of the gait when your desired end result is the goal.

Intend to Improve the Rhythm

Rhythm is your horse's language, which is characterized by repetitive movement—either the four beats of the walk, the two beats of the trot or the three beats of the canter with its moment of suspension. Concentrating on your horse's rhythm—his language—and riding in that rhythm is probably the best way to access the Zone. You find this place by tuning into that repetitive movement. Listen to your horse's footfall. You can hear it. Feel it. Your automatic, fully integrated habitual riding behavior gets incorporated into the rhythm automatically on a moment-to-moment basis. It's mesmerizing, and photos of great riders demonstrate their hypnotic expressions as you saw in Sue Blink's photo on page 93 and you can see here with Laura Graves (fig. 9.1).

When you are habitually attuned to your horse's rhythm, you are already operating in the *now*. As your horse moves in rhythm and you move with him, your motion and your aids will automatically be well-timed. The *now* changes

121

{9.1} Laura Graves rides Verdades (Diddy) at the FEI World Cup in Omaha. Clearly, Diddy knows what she wants and is happy to comply!

How Two Minds Meet:
The Mental Dynamics
of Dressage

every instant and you change with it. If you want to improve the rhythm, start with the rhythm you have and do exercises to improve it. Your *intention* is to improve the rhythm, so the chances of it happening are enormous. The power of intention can't be underestimated.

Music is a powerful method of gaining access to the Zone because it shares the element of repetitive rhythm that lures you into the space where thinking takes a back seat. Artists and writers use music to get them "in the mood" and set the tone for their works in progress.

Riders sometimes ride to "metronomed" music that is synced to the tempo of the gaits. This is of double benefit to both horse and rider because not only does the music help put you in the Zone, but the proper tempo of the music helps improve the horse's rhythm. Put that in the context of a competitive freestyle to music and you have the ability to put a whole audience in the Zone.

Intend to Improve Your Position and Your Horse's Position

Proprioception is another sense that allows you to feel the relative position of parts of your body. Concentrate on it. Are you aligned? Is your head over your hips, and are your hips over your feet? Do you feel the weight of your head in your feet? If you have a chance to ride with a mirror, check your position often. Concentrate on it in a positive way and you'll stay in the Zone. Don't let your "monkey mind" chatter in a negative way.

The word "position" implies that it is static, but I'm talking about a dynamic use of your body in motion. The "position" of your body changes every moment, but it stays relatively the same in relation to your horse. The *now* is a moving target, and learning how to stay quietly balanced on a moving horse is challenging.

For example, does your position suffer because your horse depends too much on your hands? U.S. dressage coach Debbie McDonald urges riders to "wean your horse off your hand." In other words, although we all need to use our hands, try to use your seat and legs first. Use your hands as much as necessary but as little as possible.

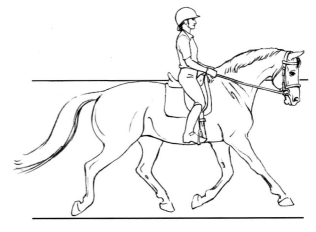

- {9.2 A} Incorrect:
  In absolute elevation, the height of the horse's neck is caused by the rider's hands. The shoulders are down because the hindquarters are disengaged.

- {9.2 B} Correct:
  In relative elevation, the height of the horse's neck is relative to the engagement of the hindquarters and the height of the shoulders. In any degree of collection, the head and neck should rise because the shoulders rise.

★ Try This

Focus on exercises that require you to use your seat and legs. In so doing, you'll increase your horse's awareness of the aids other than your hands. Depending on your horse's level, do exercises such as: turn-on-the-forehand or turn-on-the-haunches.

Play with exercises that require changing the bend. Do figure eights or transitions from shoulder-in to renvers, concentrating on your seat and leg aids and how they align your horse in left or right bend. As you confirm your "shaping aids" by transitioning from one position to another, you increase your horse's awareness of your seat and legs, and he won't rely on your hands too much. Be aware of all his awareness and everything will improve.

Be aware of your horse's position, too.

Before doing a challenging exercise, stretch your horse on a large circle, and you will increase his awareness of his relaxed, swinging back, including his neck, which falls down from the withers. Then the difficult exercise will be easier because he'll probably use his back better.

Help him focus on his hindquarters. When you get to any level of collection, the head and neck rise *because* the withers and shoulders rise (with a relaxed swinging back). The head and neck shouldn't rise when the shoulders are down (figs. 9.2 A & B).

Ride from back to front, channeling the energy from behind to the bit. Then your half-halts transfer the weight back to your horse's hindquarters. The hindquarters are out of sight but must never be out of mind. Concentrate on all these details in a positive way and fold your specific intentions into your vision. In the process, your awarenesses will silence compulsive thoughts and emotions.

Intend to Be Accurate

Riding precise figures is another form of "reaching" because you are literally orienting the horse in relation to the earth and connecting to the environment. The trajectory of your eyes finds a reference point that is outside yourself, and your aids keep your horse on the desired path. In the process, you are balancing your horse.

Following a specific line of travel is quite a left-brained issue until you know where the points are. Then you can concentrate on them positively. Riding a 20-meter circle accurately is a time-honored way to develop an ideal connection with your horse. For example, you may wish to warm up your horse on this circle with walk-trot-walk and trot-canter-trot transitions. But it only works when you're accurate so every stride can be the same. If the circle isn't accurate, consistent balance will be impossible for the horse because every step will be different.

Horses actually train us to have all these positive qualities. They train us to "Feed the Good Wolf" and be our very best selves. Horses reward us for using those behavioral keys that put us in the Zone. They teach us to be present and positive, to abandon the ego, and to reach out to feel compassion and curiosity and wonder. They teach us to concentrate, to listen, to be aware, and to care.

WHAT TO DO
– Use Cones –

IF you have trouble managing space, set up cones to help you (fig. 9.3). Cones help because you don't have to be thinking about the space as you ride. You can delegate that issue to the cones so you're free to be in your "right" mind when you're riding.

Years ago, Swedish trainer Major Anders Lindgren was known for teaching with cones. In one of his lessons, he set up an arena with cones to help his students ride the Intermediaire I test. There were a lot of cones in that arena, but they made the work easy! They helped his students be very accurate about the line of travel, which in turn, helped their horses balance. That Intermediaire test was so easy that it clarified, for me, the importance of managing space. When you ride with cones frequently, you won't need them at some point because the geometry of the arena will become innately very meaningful to you. Then you can just concentrate on the line of travel. Your intention is to be accurate and you won't need the cones. ●

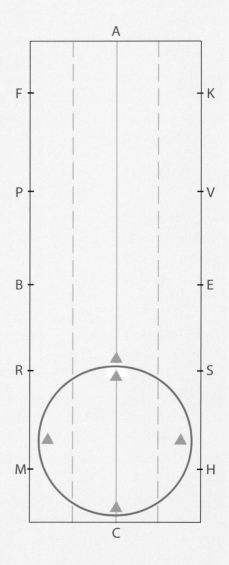

● {9.3} Exercise:
The 20-Meter Circle with Cones

How Two Minds Meet:
The Mental Dynamics
of Dressage

Essential Information About
Positive Behaviors That Take You to the Zone

✓ What you pay attention to grows. This begins with awareness and concentration on any aspect of your riding.

✓ You can fold your intentions into your concentration to improve any quality of your riding.

✓ It can be said that horses train you to "Feed the Good Wolf" and be your very best self. They reward you for abandoning your ego, being mindful, attentive, and caring.

SUMMARY 9

**PLAYFULNESS
IS THE 'RIGHT' MIND
FOR RIDING, WHICH IS MORE
ABOUT FEELING THAN THINKING.**

Playing
in the Zone

10

CHAPTER

When you're in the Zone, you can utilize techniques to maximize your success. Here are a few ideas. Maybe you can think of more.

● Muscle Memory

Learning is primarily the purview of the mind but in the horseman's case, you learn with your whole body. Be aware of how movements feel. When it feels right, take a little kinesthetic picture of it in your mind. Keep in mind that your muscles have memory, and muscle memory works for both horses and riders.

In the 1970s and 80s, Swiss rider Christine Stückelberger competed a massive and wild horse named Granat. In both 1976 and 1980, they won individual gold Olympic medals. In 1978 they won the individual gold medal at the World Championships, and in 1975 and 1977, individual gold medals in the European Championships. Granat was a great horse. Many people remember that he did the most incredible half-passes in the world. Everyone was amazed as he redefined excellence in half-passes.

Subsequently, it was even more amazing to see that Christine's younger horses could also do incredible half-passes. Hmmm. Perhaps Granat gave Christine the feel and the muscle memory for great half-passes, and she passed it on to her other horses! Then horses with great half-passes give the feel to other riders and our sport evolves positively through time until today when we can see Laura Graves and Verdades

Throughout the development of your horse, continue to exercise your muscle memory with awareness.

half-pass as she did in the Omaha FEI World Cup (see fig. 9.1, p. 122).

You can see the same phenomenon in modern riders. Charlotte Dujardin rode Valegro with incredible skill. Every movement was extraordinary, and now we see that all her other horses have the same remarkable abilities. Years ago, Kyra Kyrklund had a great horse named Matador. He had a very distinct, elegant neck. At the same time, I had a Dutch stallion in training that had the same neck. I learned that Kyra had started my horse. Her specific training actually created horses with that elegant neck.

Horses are our kinesthetic teachers. No human coach could have given Christine or Charlotte those feelings. And only those riders could then endow their future horses with the ability to move with such grandeur.

Be aware of how movements feel. Your instructor's eye on the ground is very helpful, because when a movement is good, she will say, "YES! That's it!" At the same time, you probably noticed that it felt just right, but that confirmation from the ground is very important.

How do you develop muscle memory? Remember that what you pay attention to grows. Be aware, for example, of how a perfect 20-meter circle feels. Notice how your horse balances on the outside rein. Be aware of the self-perpetuating nature of the rhythm on that circle and how much bend is required to make every step exactly the same. Concentrate on it. Take an imaginary kinesthetic photo of the feeling of what you think of as perfection. Maybe you'll replace it with a better feeling later, but for now, you'll be better able to reproduce the positive feeling if you're very aware of it.

Throughout the development of your horse, continue to exercise your muscle memory with awareness. How does a 15-meter circle feel? A 10-meter circle? How does it feel to retain that 10-meter bend on a straight line in shoulder-in? How does tracking right feel as compared with tracking left? Be aware. How can you make them comparable? The examples of how you can develop your muscle memory are endless.

● Mental Practice

Many riders have "ridden" in their imagination during a time when they couldn't *actually* ride, only to find that their skills improved dramatically during that sabbatical. This happened to me after my sophomore year in college. I desperately missed riding during that summer when I couldn't arrange it. After I returned to school for my junior year, my riding instructor wondered where in the world I had been training because my improvement was so remarkable. I had literally only ridden in my mind for months. Mental practice is a form of daydreaming or self-hypnosis that is in the *now*, even if it's just a pretend *now*. You're not thinking of the past or the future.

131

Educational studies have proven that mental practice is as influential as physical practice and can certainly boost innate talent because your improvement becomes a part of you.

Be sure that you always practice mentally for a score of 10. Your mental repetitions, unlike in real life, can be perfect. Practice doesn't make perfect. Perfect practice makes perfect, and it is much easier to be perfect in your mind. In fact, you have to conceive of that perfection before you can approach it in real life.

● Imitation and Imagination

You are only able to improve your riding if you can watch someone better than yourself—or if you can watch riders who are better in a specific way. German superstar Dorothee Schneider studies other riders and emulates aspects of their riding that she thinks will help her. You can rise above your current riding environment and set higher goals for yourself by reaching out to find a better situation to emulate.

Fortunately, the internet makes it possible to watch any top rider in the world, and those who avail themselves of that opportunity enable their improvement. Most riders don't have an excellent rider to emulate in their own barn, but they can always watch great riders online. You might identify with a specific rider, either because he or she has similar body conformation to your own, or maybe your affinity for a specific rider is for some unknown reason. Follow your gut with this, and imagine how it feels to be that rider. It will definitely improve your own riding! In Part III, I'll talk much more about

Studies have proven that mental practice is as influential as physical practice.

imitation as one of the best tools of learning (see p. 141).

Which rider do you identify with? Maybe the spirit of Ingrid Klimke's riding inspires you (fig. 10.1). Is crookedness a problem of yours? If so, check out Kyra Kyrklund's riding. She's very straight, and she's good at teaching straightness. If you study her riding, you'll figure out why. Then pretend you're Kyra!

These great riders are wonderful role models. Let one of them be your imaginary mentor who will improve your weaknesses.

Imagination also has everything to do with goal-setting, and I talk much more about that in Part Three when we talk about accountability (see p. 182). Riders learn better when they are accountable by being tested at a horse show. Imagine yourself riding every step of your ideal ride at the next horse show. Or imagine yourself riding at a clinic or a riding lesson. Make it good!

As an aside, it's human nature to always imagine the future as either better or worse than the present. Be aware of how you're shaping your future. Make it a good one!

{10.1} Here Ingrid Klimke is riding SAP Hale Bob. Ingrid's spirit inspires many riders. If you're one of them, watch her often and then take it a step farther. Imagine that you are Ingrid Klimke. Pull on her boots, adopt her posture, and wear her joyous facial expression. It can't hurt!

Imagination and Humor

Lendon Gray once taught a pony rider in one of her many Dressage4Kids clinics. During a break in her lesson, Lendon asked her, "Now, would you rather I think, 'Ohhh, what a cute little pony rider.' Or would you rather I think, 'Wow! I feel like I'm watching a future Olympian!'"

The rider agreed that she would much rather be regarded as a future Olympian, and off she went on her pony to finish her lesson. During the rest of the lesson, much of Lendon's commentary was, "Ohhhh, what a cute little pony rider!" As a result of Lendon's imagination and humor, this pony rider looked like a champion within 45 minutes!

At a show on the following weekend, the rider went to pick up her test sheet, and the judge, who had absolutely no knowledge of the lesson with Lendon, had written at the bottom of the test, "I feel like I'm watching a future Olympian."

This powerful story demonstrates not only the power of Lendon's playful imagination and use of humor, but also the strong possibility that some serious ESP was going on at that horse show! ●

> *Clear intention is the mental equivalent of clear physical aids, and it is powerfully transformative.*

Planning for your future takes you *out* of the *now*. That's okay! It requires honest assessment, including acknowledging some negative aspects of your riding. It requires making a plan for improvement, perhaps looking at a timeframe, goal-setting, and accountability.

● Intention

We've already talked about folding your intentions into your riding. Remember what Conrad Schumacher told his students, "You must have the WILL!" He was usually talking about the rider's mental commitment to, for example, a line of sequence flying changes. His voice boomed throughout the arena, making it clear that the riders must make *their* intentions extremely clear to their horses.

Clear intention is the mental equivalent of clear physical aids and it is powerfully transformative. How does the Power of Intent work? Is it about Extrasensory Perception—ESP? Is it mind reading? Are brain waves like radio waves? Does the rider's mental commitment merely result in clearer physical aids? Or is it all of these things? Regardless, riders need to be very clear about what they want. To have clear intent, you must *know* precisely what result you want and what the correct aids are to achieve it.

You must know the *one* thing you want. You can't want a lot of things at once. If your mind is saying, *I need to improve this and this and this,* your horse won't understand the multiple aspects of your intentions. He will be confused and possibly become inattentive. Decide the *one* most underlying quality that needs to be addressed and concentrate on that positively.

Excellent instructors do this masterfully. They find the *one* most underlying issue and help the rider improve it. Then they identify the *next* most underlying issue, and they help the rider improve that, until bit by bit, the rider is having a "great ride." This was by design, and if you don't have an excellent instructor helping from the wings, you can try to do it for yourself by concentrating on sequence (read more about sequence on p. 150).

★ Try This

Exercises to Clarify Your Intentions

1. With your left brain, *decide* what quality you would like to improve most. It might, for example, be the connection from the inside leg to the outside rein.

2. Understand the prerequisites for this quality with your left brain. Know that your horse can't go to the outside rein if you don't have *flexion to the inside* because the flexion decides which the *inside* is, and by default, which side the *outside* is. Know that *your line of travel has to be accurate* or your horse will lose his balance every step of the way.

3. *Concentrate* on the action plan step by step, moment to moment. In the present, in the *now*, in the Zone. Your horse must clearly know your *intent,* and if you're concentrating on it, he will know it and be able to concentrate on it too. Both of you will be able to feel because you're both in the Zone.

135

4. *Praise* your horse if his performance is even a little bit better.

For the next exercise, clarify your intention by asking your horse verbally—out loud—for what you want. For example, as in the previous example, perhaps you want a better connection to the outside rein.

1. If you're tracking left, the first step is to ask him to flex to the left. "Please flex left." This will clarify your intention and actually remind you to ask with your physical aids—your inside left seat/leg and wrist (not your arm).

2. When he's flexed left to your satisfaction, be sure he isn't over-flexed or over-bent in the neck (from using your arm). Then ask him out loud, "Please step toward the outside right rein. Put some weight in your outside rein." Be aware of the rhythm and use your left leg in a way that sends energy in the direction of the bit on the right. If he's very slightly bent left, the right bit is probably almost directly in front of you, and your right rein needs to be receptive—listening—not talking.

As an aside, have you ever seen a horse performing well when the rider was asking with the wrong aids? Of course you have! It happens all the time. Why? It's the power of intent. The horse understood the rider's intent even though the rider's physical skill was either inadequate or the rider didn't know how to ask.

● **Expectation**

After intention, comes expectation. If you've made your mental intention and your physical aids clear, then the competent and *consequent* (see p. 29) rider *expects* the correct outcome. The less competent rider *hopes* for the correct outcome.

Hope, for all its positive features, is in the realm of wishful thinking. I *hope* my horse will win his class, but of course, my hoping for it doesn't increase the chances of it happening. *Belief* is based on some factual experience and is in the realm of *positive thinking*. I *believe* my horse will win because I have trained him to understand his task. You believe you'll give your horse a positive schooling session because you usually do. *Expectation* is based on a lot of factual experience and is in the realm of *powerful thinking*. You expect your horse will have a positive schooling session because you almost always do. There is tremendous power in *intent* and *expectation*. And there is a simplicity to these powers that is beyond the complications of *how*. It doesn't involve *how* to do a shoulder-in or *how* to ask for a shorter or a longer stride.

In the riding world, if you're a competent rider with clear aids and clear intent, you can *expect* your horse to do a shoulder-in when you ask for it. You expect your horse to shorten the stride or jump the fence. You don't hope he's going to do it.

Can you revamp your hopes and beliefs into expectations? Let's look at the common request for a precise canter depart at a given marker:

- Rider A *hopes* the horse will canter (*wishful thinking*).

- Rider B *believes* the horse will canter (*positive thinking*).

- Rider C *expects* the horse to canter (powerful thinking that usually creates reality).

Rider D is worried she won't be done in time to get to the office for an important board meeting (*confused thinking*). Who knows what message the horse is getting from this? Concentration on the desired outcome is a requirement for riding.

How High Are Your Goals?

About 45 years ago I learned an unlikely lesson at a horse show. My horse was stabled in one of those portable stalls with canvas between your horse and the horses next to and behind you. One quiet evening, I was cleaning my horse's stall when I heard a man talking to his horse in the stall behind me.

"Tomorrow we'll dance," he said, presumably to his horse. "It will be like poetry. Harmonious and beautiful."

I was stunned. This man's goals were so far beyond mine. My goal was to stay on top, and he was actually planning on creating something beautiful. Who was that man? I had to find out who had given me this tremendous mental adjustment.

It was a man who later represented the United States in the 1992 Barcelona Olympic Games, Michael Poulin.●

(However, to give Rider D a little credit, her thoughts might actually be more important than those of Riders A, B, and C, but she shouldn't be riding. When you only have a half-hour to ride, make it a good half-hour then get off.)

What happens in each of these scenarios? How does a horse experience his rider's hope for a shoulder-in? How does he experience the rider's belief that a shoulder-in will happen? We can assume he would experience *belief* more clearly than *hope*. And we can assume he would find *expectation* even more influential than belief and far more powerful than hope. Does the horse experience the rider's intention and expectation mentally or is the intent of the rider embedded in the physical aid? Or both? Notice that expectation is based on real life success with, in this case, canter departs. It's not all in your head. You have to actually be able to do it with competence.

Why Some Riders Excel

All experienced riding instructors have had some students who excel while others remain forever struggling for average. All of these students obviously have the same instructor and many have comparable horses and comparable talent. Why? Perhaps some enable and empower themselves more. They imagine a different future with higher expectations. Serious goal-setting requires that you get out of the *now* and see a glowing future beyond the present. It's true that some people spend too much time in the *now*. Perhaps the rider who excels spends time planning a bright future. I'll discuss this further in the section on accountability (see p. 182).

Perhaps the rider who excels is more consequent and particular about getting a specific obedient response as a result of her specific aid. Perhaps the rider is more persistent and able to "layer her intentions" into her concentration or perhaps she gives her physical aids more clearly. Perhaps the rider who doesn't progress spends too much time in the Comfort Zone (see p. 71). It's impossible to say because every rider is different, but it's probably safe to say that as more and more riders become technically correct and progress, eventually winning will become the province of the mind—and that mind includes your emotions.

Behind every communication with a horse lies a rider's emotion, which can be boiled down to either a positive emotion or a negative one. Maybe the successful rider is just more positive. The truth is that the rider who excels probably does so for a number of reasons. ●

*How Two Minds Meet:
The Mental Dynamics
of Dressage*

Expectation, Confidence, and Ego

Expectation and *confidence* are close cousins because they are both borne of real experience. When you honestly expect the best because of past experience, you probably feel confident. Your confidence isn't driven by ego, but rather it is created organically by experience.

The ego is boastful in nature, so in entering the Zone, you have to leave your ego at the door.

Essential Information About Playing in the Zone

When in the Zone, you can utilize certain techniques that maximize your success. Use of these techniques also helps put you in the Zone and keeps you there. For example:

✓ Awareness of **muscle memory** will help your conscious habits become unconscious.

✓ *Mental practice* with excellence will help you reproduce that excellence physically.

✓ *Imitation* is one of the most powerful forms of learning. Having a mentor to emulate enables you to set your goals higher.

✓ *Imagination* helps you look to a brighter future and enables you to practice the other techniques.

✓ *Intentions:* When these are clear to you and to your horse, chances of achieving success is high. Learn ways to clarify your intentions.

✓ *Expectation* is a powerful tool. When you *expect* a desired result, your chances of success are much higher than if you simply believe or hope for that success.

SUMMARY 10

The Principles of Learning

RIDERS CAN HELP THEIR PERSONAL LEARNING CURVES BY STUDYING AND IMPLEMENTING BASIC LEARNING PRINCIPLES.

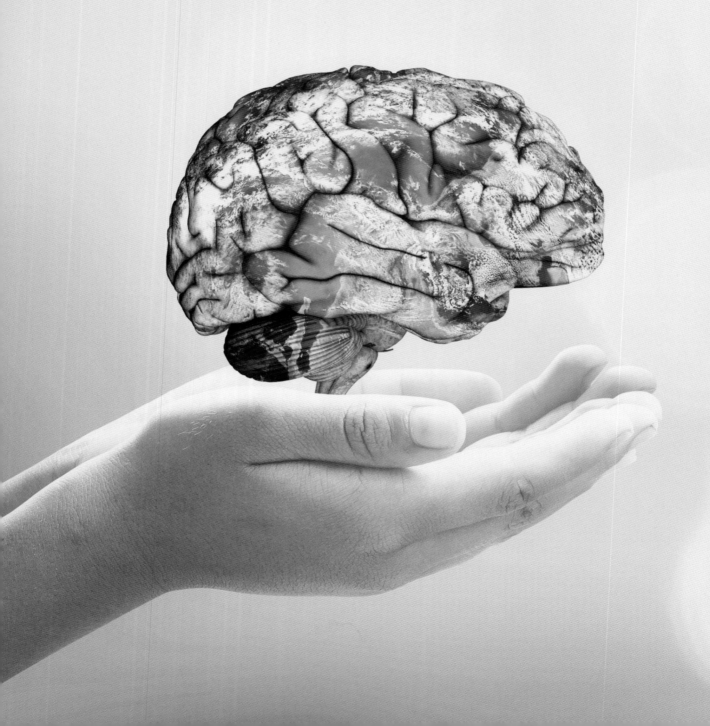

11

Use Your Whole Brain to Enhance Growth for You and Your Horse

11

Teachers study educational psychology and explore "principles of learning" that enable students to learn faster as well as increase understanding and retention. Although teachers might seem to be the best group to apply these principles, ultimately, the responsibility lies with the learner who, in this case, is the rider. Riders can help their personal learning curves by studying and implementing those same basic principles.

These principles can be applied to any learning situation—whether the learner is in first grade or riding First Level, whether she is doing post-graduate work or Grand Prix.

You'll use both your right- and left-brained skills to implement these ideas. There are Nine Principles listed in the pages that follow, but maybe you can think of more.

● 1. The Principle of Imitation and Social Learning

Most of us are inclined to think of riding as an individual sport, but in truth, we need other riders and trainers around us. Social learning theory posits that we learn primarily from observing others. Social learning involves four steps: We pay attention (to our role model); we remember (retention); and we copy or imitate (reproduction) because we have motivation to be like the role model.

Learning to ride and train horses is no different. We can't learn to ride horses in a vacuum. Imitation is the most natural form and the

Social learning theory posits that we learn primarily from observing others.

most powerful form of learning. It can, however, work for you or against you. Riders who are able to watch a great rider on a daily basis have an incredible edge, and those who watch riders with flawed technique or poor attitudes almost inevitably follow suit. Those who understand the power of imitation—and the inevitability of it—have the slogan, "Never watch bad riding." Bad riding is as contagious as good riding.

In this digital age, anyone can take the time to watch great riders every day of the week. Remember the story of Jessica Morgan who excelled because she made a habit of watching great European riders online (see p. 81). Make the power of imitation work for you instead of against you. That doesn't mean you can't respect those who don't have the perfection gene, but if you want to train your horse as well as possible, find a mentor to watch—someone you aspire to look like. A picture is, in fact, more powerful than any number of well-chosen words.

Years ago before there were many good trainers in our country, U.S. Dressage Team rider Shelly Francis was working on developing her own riding style with determination and perseverance.

She lived in rural, northern New England long before the years when she was vying for a spot on the Team. Her horses were stabled at a farm with an arena, good footing, and an empty judge's booth, but she was without mirrors and without help most of the time.

Henry Wynmalen's book, however, was her bible. It was called *Dressage: A Study of the Finer Points of Riding* and was first published in 1899. She put her little brother in that judge's booth with Wynmalen's book, opened it to her favorite photograph and told him, "Now, just tell me when I look like that picture!" Those New Englanders had (and still have) grit and determination that can outweigh any number of difficulties. Shelly Francis is one of them. In 1996, Shelly was second alternate for the U.S. Olympic team with Pikant. In 1997, the pair won the USDF Grand Prix Horse of the Year and in 1998, they represented the United States at the World Equestrian Games in Rome. Twenty years later, riding Doktor and Danilo, she amassed top placings at the Grand Prix in Europe as well as in the United States.

Shelly's story began in the 1980s, and at that time, Americans had almost no chance in the equestrian sport of dressage. Why was it so hopeless? After all, each of those Europeans had only one lifetime, and each of us has only one lifetime.

Why were European lives more productive? *Because of this principle of imitation.* Our national dressage IQ was very low. We had no dressage culture, so there was no one to imitate, and technology was nowhere near what it is today. The Europeans had been breeding horses for dressage for many decades. The children of German

145

part three / chapter 11
Use Your Whole Brain to Enhance
Growth for You and Your Horse

riders Georg and Inge Theodorescu, Reiner and Ruth Klimke, and many others were playing in the arena sandboxes at the feet of their parents' piaffing and passaging footsteps. Those children included German Olympians Ingrid Klimke and Monica Theodorescu. Monica subsequently served as coach of the German team. There are too many examples to list. The dressage culture was deeply ingrained in Europe, and there were probably no dressage riders in the United States with that same degree of skill, never mind the layers of understanding that make up a complex culture of dressage horsemen.

As a result, the search for appropriate dressage horses in the United States began as a great exodus to Europe. What used to be a few determined riders going to Europe to ride with a mentor was now a number too high to count. Riders realized that their American horses were bred to run fast, and it wasn't that difficult to import a European horse that was born to do the job. In Europe you could find hundreds of Warmbloods for sale within the same geographical space of New England. The European culture was deep and rich. The equestrian population was dense; there were extremely competent riders everywhere. Not only were they thoroughly steeped in the finest equestrian culture, they often had an attitude of joy about their riding, which was adopted by their children and their grandchildren. Americans who actually settled in Europe could experience that culture firsthand; they could *see* the path, and they were on it!

Dressage has become a much more global sport now. There are genuine experts on other continents; however, Europeans may enjoy top

Think about the culture of your barn, and think about how you contribute to that culture. Is there a team spirit?

billing for years to come because their training barns, sales barns, riding clubs, and shows are still in close proximity to one another, and their culture still runs deep. They feel quite comfortable on the top podium at the biggest events.

Learning happens most easily in social situations such as Europe enjoys. The culture of the Aachen Horse Show, for example, reflects the excitement that comes when the best dressage, show jumping, and eventing riders, along with the best drivers in the world convene. The audiences are educated and socially engaged throughout the week. Whereas the competition is keen, friendship and camaraderie abound. There are countless riding clubs and fabulous horse shows in Europe. In this country, Wellington, Florida, has a similar culture of friendly competition and love of learning. Other centers are developing around the world, but the sport in Europe is still the most dense.

The Barn Culture

Learning to ride is very personal. Dressage trainers differ tremendously even though they all tend to read the same dressage books and magazines and hear from the same experts. We all tend to ride our horses a bit in the same way that we live our lives. For that reason, the choice of a teacher or a mentor is very personal. Each trainer and instructor has a system of values or a culture that either feels right or does not feel right to the student. It's like choosing a college or a spouse or a dog. We each are drawn to whatever "fits" with our own values and personal preferences. The culture of a stable might be fun or intellectual, driven toward competition, strict, laid back, or a combination of some of these qualities and others too. But the healthy culture always includes a measure of encouragement.

Think about the culture of your barn, and think about how you contribute to that culture. Is there a *team spirit*? Are you all cheering for one another? When that's the case, riders don't shrink in self-consciousness. They can ride honestly, thoughtfully, from the heart and in the moment. A culture of "well-wishing" is tremendously powerful, and some farms reflect this principle strongly. Riders should never experience the debilitating ill-will that results when someone is critiquing negatively from the corner of the arena.

At shows, the power of that "well-wishing" grows exponentially, allowing each rider and horse to do as well as possible. When the power of well-wishing is there, riders are free to concentrate and communicate confidently with the horse. Then the horse, in turn, can concentrate and communicate confidently with his rider. This maximizes the chances for success. Remember that horses should bring out our very best selves.

The owner of a famous dressage and jumping stable in Germany was once asked to tell the secret of the success at his farm. He said he thought it was because his riders and stable workers had lunch together every day. They sat down together in a relaxed atmosphere and could talk freely and comfortably about whatever was on their minds. That simple tradition developed strong camaraderie.

The success of the United States bronze-medal-winning dressage team at the 2016 Olympic Games in Rio was at least partially because of the team camaraderie. The riders and the individuals who supported these riders maximized their chances of success by being mutually supportive team players.

Social Learning TIPS

- ✓ Imitation is the most effective form of learning, and although riding is often considered an individual sport, it's difficult to do alone.

- ✓ Make constant efforts to be your own ideal rider by consciously searching for role models.

- ✓ Be aware of the culture in your barn and encourage "well-wishing" within it.

- ✓ Horses love to be in groups, so look for opportunities to ride together with others.

147

part three / chapter 11
Use Your Whole Brain to Enhance
Growth for You and Your Horse

How Two Minds Meet:
The Mental Dynamics
of Dressage

Social Learning for Horses

Horses don't admire the elevation and swing of another horse and try to imitate it, but they do puff up and show off when another horse walks in the arena. Riders can use that to find another layer of expression in the horse's work. Is the shoulder-in inclined to be a little flat? Try it when a new horse walks in the arena, and your horse might be inclined to give you a little more power and lift. Then maybe you can reproduce that on your own later.

As you know, horses are very social creatures, and as herd animals, they're meant to be in a group. It would behoove us to put them in groups more often. Horses love drill teams and quadrilles. When on a hack, horses love being with a group or riding in tandem. Horses with exposure to other horses on their hack days are almost always more enthusiastic and willing to work on the following day. Riding in groups is sometimes easy to implement, but some of us should just think of it more often (fig. 11.1). ●

● {11.1} Horses are herd animals and do well in groups. Hacking, riding tandem or working in quadrilles is exhilarating for them, and they're almost always more willing to work on the following day.

149

part three / chapter 11
Use Your Whole Brain to Enhance
Growth for You and Your Horse

2. The Principle of Readiness

The Principle of Readiness is all about "sequence," and it applies to all learning. Barring extenuating circumstances, no one was ever a star in First Grade and just couldn't handle Second Grade. And the same can be said of First Level and Second Level in dressage. The fact of the matter is, if you do First Level poorly, you won't do Second Level well, and Third Level will be ugly. Conversely, if you concentrate on the most basic level, the next levels are manageable and relatively easy. In most European countries, riders aren't allowed to progress to a higher-level test in competition until they've achieved an acceptable standard at their current level.

The skills required in the standard dressage tests are presented sequentially. These tests represent the collective genius of decades of great horsemen, and in the early days of dressage in this country, before we had ever heard of the Training Scale, competitors like Lendon Gray used the tests as a guide in the training of horses. The tests told her, *First your horse should be able to do this, and now this—and now that your horse can do that, you can try this.* Lendon was obviously on the right track, and as she continued on down that path to the Olympic Games and beyond, she developed a deep understanding of the reasons *why* the sequence worked so well. That's one reason why she's such a good teacher. She learned this sport from the bottom up, step by step.

Do you know some people who are very talented riders but aren't very good teachers? Talented riders don't always make good teachers because they didn't necessarily learn step by step by step—the slow way. They didn't necessarily need to realize what they were doing sequentially. They may never have had to hammer out the details in an intellectual way. The best teachers have gone through the process themselves. They have made mistakes, and they understand the process, the sequence, and the pitfalls.

In addition to the dressage tests, the Training Scale, also known as the Pyramid of Training, guides us in the sequential training of horses (fig. 11.2). This Training Scale describes the *qualities* that should be present as the horse does the exercises through the levels. For example,

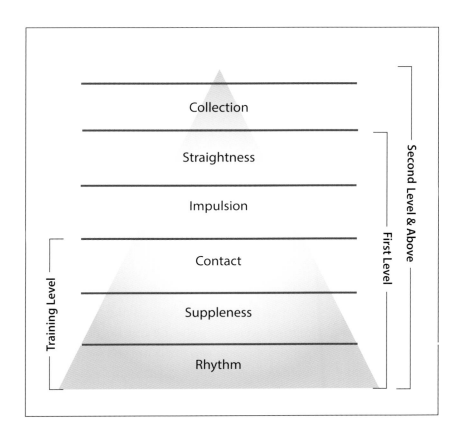

In the diagram, from bottom to top:

Rhythm

Suppleness

Contact

Impulsion

Straightness

Collection

Training Level

First Level

Second Level & Above

● {11.2} The Training Scale, also known as the Pyramid of Training sequentially describes the qualities that trainers should work on when developing their horses. It is every trainer's bible. (See also the official USDF rendition of the illustration on p. 198.)

the horse at Training Level should maintain good *rhythm,* he should be *supple* and *relaxed*, and he should accept *contact* with the bit. When you combine the qualities of the Training Scale with the exercises in each of the dressage levels, you have a pretty accurate guide for how your horse should be trained sequentially.

Going back to those dressage tests, each level has a "Purpose," which is printed on the front of the test. And the purposes show how the qualities of the Training Scale should evolve ideally within each level. In the Appendix, you can read about the purposes of each level (see p. 197). Always keep the purpose in mind when you're competing. It's good to know what you're supposed to be proving—not only to the judge but to your horse, too.

part three / chapter 11
Use Your Whole Brain to Enhance
Growth for You and Your Horse

Great Teachers Are like Scientists

Many years ago, George Morris, who will forever be regarded as the father of hunt seat equitation, offered clinics for teachers in New Jersey. At one of those clinics, I learned why his riders were so successful. His attention to detail was unparalleled. He noticed every strength and every weakness of each horse and rider, and in his mind he could manage the countless interrelated factors. They were somehow organized sequentially in his head so he always had the right exercise (of many) to address the underlying medley of circumstances. Equitation was a science to George, and that made him a genius at teaching.

Art begins where science leaves off. Understanding equitation in any discipline is technical, scientific, and sequential. Those who master it enter the realm of artists. Great teachers understand sequence so thoroughly that lessons seem simple—only because they are presented sequentially.

The ideal instructor might watch her student riding and see seven things she wants to work on, but she knows which one needs to be addressed first. She knows the most underlying problem. Then when that's taken care of, she knows what to do next. And so on. This extremely educated instruction makes riding easy for the student, and when a rider is immersed in a culture of this sequential learning (as opposed to having a lesson here and there), it makes a permanent, logistical imprint.

Why is it important for the instructor to be able to find the underlying problem? Because not only is learning most efficient and productive when it is sequential, but riders can only focus on one thing at a time. If the instructor sees seven

No one was ever a star in First Grade and just couldn't handle Second Grade. And the same can be said of First Level and Second Level in dressage.

problems, she should ideally only focus on one—the main problem—the underlying issue that will improve everything else. Of course, it's not always that simple because sometimes you **have** to think about more than one thing at a time. For example, sometimes you have to concentrate on bend, but your figure—the circle or the serpentine—also has to be accurate.

Doing Two Things at a Time

The rider can only focus on one thing at a time, but sometimes she needs to focus on more than one issue. For example, when the rider is improving bend, she needs to be on a *precise* circle—whether it's a 20-meter Training Level circle or a 10-meter Second Level circle. If the horse loses his line of travel on the circle, he will inevitably lose the bend and balance along with it.

So the rider needs to concentrate on both the accuracy of the circle and the bending aids. While she gets the feel of how to shape her horse in 20-meter bend with her seat, leg, and rein aids, the instructor can simplify the horse and rider's task exponentially by (you guessed it by now) using cones to define the circle points (see p. 126). The rider can perpetually point her aids (and, therefore, her horse) to the next circle point and be in a position of trying to do a specific and positive task. Without those cones, many riders aren't able to ride a correct 20-meter circle, and as a result, the horse loses his balance frequently. Then the rider usually ends up telling the horse what *not* to do instead of what *to* do. And we all know how well that works…not at all!

> ## ★ Try This

With the help of the cones, the rider is free to experiment and try different combinations of aids to establish the bend consistently. Later, the rider will be able to develop a 20- or 10-meter bend without the use of cones. Sequentially, once horse and rider can manage the 20-meter circle in both directions, they are able to work on a serpentine. Most riders find this figure very challenging, but the only add-on difficulty is the change of direction, which is simple in theory but not so easy in practice (fig. 11.3).

Exercise in Mastering the Serpentine

Visualize how the 20 by 60-meter arena accommodates three 20-meter circles (see p. 154). To ride the serpentine, you're going to ride three half circles with changes of direction.

1. From working trot rising, track right and begin your serpentine at C. Ride your first half circle like this: Your horse is slightly flexed right, in front of the right leg and feeling solid in the left rein. Feel the arc of your horse's body (because of your right leg) conform with the arc of the 20-meter circle from C to the first circle point on the long side.

2. As you leave the long side, half-halt in 20-meter bend and shorten your horse's trot strides in preparation to walk near the quarterline.

153

part three / chapter 11
Use Your Whole Brain to Enhance
Growth for You and Your Horse

3. As you walk from quarterline to quarterline, change your horse's flexion and bend. As you cross the centerline, ask him to be in front of your new inside (left) leg and fill up the right rein, establishing 20-meter bend to the left that conforms with the circle that goes toward E.

4. At the next quarterline, ask for working trot rising and ride toward E. After E, repeat Steps 2 and 3. During the walk between the two quarterlines, prepare for and establish right bend putting your horse in front of the new inside (right) leg and into the left rein to finish the serpentine at A with 20-meter bend to the right.

If you're like most riders, your horse "stuck" to the rail at A and C, benignly taking you into the corners. He also stuck to the rail at the circle points making the circle into an irregular oblong or oval, requiring you to bend him more than 20-meters worth to get him back on track. Remember that this exercise is easy when the bend is the same throughout, making the balance ideal. The outside aids are the turning aids. *Use* them to keep your horse on the line of travel.

If the serpentine is too difficult for any reason, do the whole exercise in walk.

When the trot serpentine is easy, try it without the transition to walk. Make the transition before the centerline *almost* to walk. Then when the horse is supple, and the contact is good, you can ask your horse to change the flexion and bend in trot as you cross the centerline. Riders who keep sequence in mind can usually find the easiest way for the horse.

● {11.3} Exercise in Mastering the Serpentine

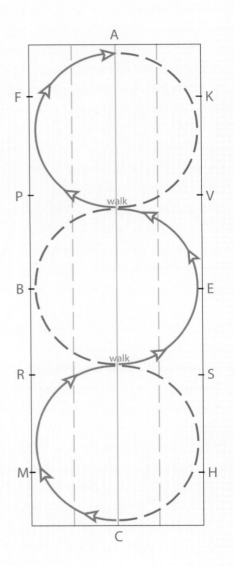

Exercise for the Shoulder-In

When the Second Level rider wonders why the shoulder-in is difficult, it is usually because the 10-meter bend isn't true. This is another example of the importance of sequence. It's very difficult to do an accurate 10-meter circle because the aids have to be working perfectly, and when the 10-meter circle is not correct, the rider certainly isn't going to be able to manage the add-on difficulty of retaining 10-meter bend on a straight line as is required in shoulder-in. That's a simple example of how an understanding of sequence helps your training. The circle has to be good before the shoulder-in can be good.

To help with the 10-meter circle, you can use cones, or you can ask a reliable person to put you on a 5-meter longe line. The person with the longe line simply needs to be a reliable post and let you figure out how to use your aids so the horse fills up the rein correctly on the entire 10-meter circle. Most horses will be inclined to fall in on one part of the circle and fall out at another point.

Even if it's far from perfect, go forward on a straight line very frequently and change directions. Don't do more than two 10-meter circles in walk or trot at a time. Do what you can do, and save the rest for tomorrow and the next day.

Underlying Factors are Primary

Whereas dressage tests and the Training Scale provide a sequence for training, there are other factors that are sequentially even more basic.

Before you can expect rhythm, suppleness, relaxation, and good contact in Training Level, Test 1, the responsible rider checks out the deeper underlying factors:

- The physical comfort of the horse: soundness in wind and limb, comfort in the back, health of teeth and eyes, and all other aspects of bodily comfort.

- The mental comfort of the horse—he's probably not going to be relaxed and rhythmic when the flapping tent is bothering him. Either you ride in a different place, or he makes peace with the flapping tent.

- You should know the horse's degree of fitness and whether or not the horse might be fatigued. A wisely chosen light day of work, a hack or a day off for the tired horse might prevent injury.

- Well-fitting tack: the bridle and bit need to be appropriate, the correct size, and adjusted correctly. The saddle also needs to fit the horse well and distribute your weight correctly. Otherwise you can't sit correctly and the horse will be uncomfortable and out of balance.

- A rider sometimes has outside personal worries. For example, a mom might be concerned about a work-related worry or what she should plan for her kid's birthday party. A rider who is a doctor might be waiting for a call from a patient. All of these situations are honestly more important than the quality of the half-pass. The great instructor's automatic instinct is to go for

155

part three / chapter 11
Use Your Whole Brain to Enhance
Growth for You and Your Horse

WHAT TO DO

– A Question of Sequence –

Here's a situation that involves a number of problems. In what sequence do you think the problems might best be solved?

- *Your horse isn't forward.*
- *Your saddle doesn't sit right—it's too low in the cantle.*
- *You are behind the motion.*
- *Your horse isn't on the bit.*

A horse can't be on the bit if he isn't forward, and he might not have a forward attitude because his saddle doesn't fit right and his rider isn't going with the motion. Maybe you're having trouble going with the motion because the saddle doesn't sit right. Fix the problems in this order:

1. *Even if it's a short-term fix with shims, try to balance your saddle so the horse is more comfortable and you can balance in the saddle.*

2. *With the improved balance of the saddle, you might be better equipped to go with the motion of your horse. Your base of support should "support" your upper body.*

3. *At this point, you have a right to expect your horse to go forward, and you can send energy through the topline to the bit.*

4. *Finally, your horse will, in theory, be on the bit.*

There are comparable sequential issues within every riding session. The best teachers are able to find the underlying issue and attend to the other issues sequentially. If you ride on your own, try to train yourself to keep sequence in mind. ●

How Two Minds Meet:
The Mental Dynamics
of Dressage

the basic underlying quality that will improve everything else. If the instructor knows about the mom's concern, then it's best to wait and improve the half-pass on another day.

Some problems can be solved by paying attention to the Laws of Nature that are absolute and cannot be refuted. For example, *gravity* is a force that all top riders use to their benefit. Everyone knows about gravity, but many riders don't utilize gravity to help themselves be grounded and effective. When the rider's knee lifts and pinches and her heel is up, the law of gravity can easily intervene to fix that problem, but the rider has to let go of the saddle and allow that to happen.

Centrifugal force is another Law of Nature that can't be denied. On a circle, the rider *will* be thrown to the outside unless she's anchoring herself (with the help of gravity) to the inside. Great teachers help their riders utilize Laws of Nature because there's not much sense in arguing with Mother Nature.

There are probably more underlying factors that are specific to your horse. It helps to be aware.

Layers of Understanding

Have you ever had an "Aha!" moment regarding something you thought you already understood? Sometimes when a rider has an "Aha!" moment, the teacher thinks, *I've been saying that for the last six months!* But the experienced teacher knows that the student wasn't ready to understand. There was suddenly a place for the rider to put that piece of information—like a jigsaw piece that finally falls into place. A visiting clinician can often explain a concept in a slightly different way that suddenly "clicks" for the student and the jigsaw puzzle becomes a bit more complete. The learning of every skill happens in layers.

For example:

- The canter depart can simply be a means of getting into canter so you can ride faster and cover more ground.

- Later, you learn that you can do a depart that's prompt and obedient.

- Even later, you learn to do a depart in which the horse reaches for the bit and uses his back correctly instead of stiffening.

- And even later, you actually feel the weight-bearing moment of the hind leg in the depart and the horse stays supple and round.

- Now, you might do a depart that is so straight that the horse could easily do a flying change to the counter lead in the next moment.

- Then the unity is such that your legs feel like they are the same as horse's hind legs!

These are *layers* of understanding within "canter depart," and other skills develop in layers, too. As a student you can finally "get" a concept, but realize that you've been told that many times, but you weren't quite ready to have that piece of the puzzle fit in so perfectly.

part three / chapter 11
Use Your Whole Brain to Enhance
Growth for You and Your Horse

Learn About Theory

A task is always easier when you understand the reasoning behind it. Try to educate yourself in theory, because it explains the whys, whens, and wheres. Instructors who are not good at teaching theory should guide their riders toward books that explain it. That theoretical reasoning is sequential and is what makes dressage theory simple and easy to understand. That doesn't mean it's easy in practice, but it's easier when you understand. Then your aids come from a very clear place. Training horses with their countless variables is not easy, but understanding the sequential "ideal" simplifies it. Good teaching is always simple and sequential. If people thought riding was so complicated that you need a high IQ and incredible athletic ability, they would quit before they began. So simplify with sequence.

It's worth noting that wishing doesn't always make a thing so. For example, sequentially, the first two qualities of the Training Scale are **rhythm** and **relaxation/suppleness**. The problem is that you can't actually **make** a horse go in a relaxed rhythm. Sometimes it's hard enough to make yourself relax, let alone another being. You need to help your horse find that relaxed rhythm through suppling exercises such as circles, figure eights, leg-yields, and serpentines. The point is that the work can't always be strictly sequential, but it always serves you to keep the sequential process very firmly in your mind, because in the end, that's the only way. By the time the horse gets to the Grand Prix, he should be more rhythmic and supple than he was at each of the lower levels.

···· *Readiness and Sequence* TIPS ····

✓ *Learning is most effective when it is sequential. For example, children who have been to First Grade, generally don't find Second Grade difficult. The same is true of First Level and Second Level.*

✓ *Great teachers are like scientists because they understand the sequences of training horses and riders, and they are skilled at teaching the most basic, underlying skills first.*

✓ *Because instructors have a thorough understanding of the process, they are good at spotting the underlying problems. The most underlying problem might be a horsemanship concern such as soundness, comfort of the tack or worries of the rider.*

✓ *The standard dressage tests and the Training Scale (the Pyramid of Training) clarify the ideal sequence for training horses.*

✓ *Students who are immersed in the program of a good instructor excel beyond those who take lessons here and there.*

✓ *Understanding of sequence requires thorough study of dressage theory.*

3. The Principle of Practice and Repetition

Malcolm Gladwell's book *Outliers* (Back Bay Books, 2011) is a study of people who succeed. What made Bill Gates, Steve Jobs, the Beatles and countless others reach extreme success? Were they simply geniuses? Perhaps, but Gladwell says that IQ and talent only predict success to a point. He proposes that there is a more compelling factor for all of those mentioned in his book: Their area of success was an obsession to them, so these "outliers" loved their obsession so completely that they didn't look upon pursuit of these obsessions as "work." They practiced within their respective fields passionately and tirelessly, and they became standouts in those fields because they were totally immersed. We're told that it takes at least 10,000 experiences of a skill before becoming extremely competent. So was it genius and talent or was it the endless repetitive practice that made the greats so great? Certainly tireless practice in a pursuit that each of them loved was a strong factor.

How do you imagine your 10,000th shoulder-in is going to be in comparison to your first or your 100th? It is not likely to look like the one in the photo on page 160 (fig. 11.4). The first ones will not be good. How can they be? It's unreasonable to expect success without practice. This is like polishing boots. A working student once said, "What am I doing wrong? These boots aren't getting shiny." The answer, "You're not doing anything wrong. You're just not done." A watched pot tells the same story. There's nothing wrong with the heat source; it just hasn't been on the stove long enough to boil.

Avoid Avoidance

In life, it's human nature to avoid things that we can't do well. It's related to the negativity bias we discussed on page 96. We love the things we do well and dislike areas of weakness. It is human nature to avoid exercises that are difficult.

A rider might avoid the honest training of downward transitions because they are difficult. That's the opposite of a training mentality though. Always give your horse small challenges that will help him learn and grow.

159

part three / chapter 11
Use Your Whole Brain to Enhance
Growth for You and Your Horse

How Two Minds Meet:
The Mental Dynamics
of Dressage

{11.4} Dutch rider Marlies van Baalen, over many years, has been practicing shoulder-in with many horses. She's surely done more than 10,000 shoulders-in. Here, she's riding Poseidon who has also had lots of practice!

The areas in which we don't excel are the very holes we need to fill. People who excel are anxious to fill these holes, to iron out the things they dislike until they have mastered them. If the leg-yield to the left is problematic, the diligent trainer is aware of needing to improve it. Practice will be a part of the plan.

A working student was asked what she wanted to concentrate on during her lesson, and she said "That serpentine that I hate with the simple changes on the centerline." That's the spirit! Iron out the things you hate. Don't let the natural tendency for avoidance get in your way. Within your level, practice the hard things.

Meaningful Repetition

Don't be too afraid of "drilling" because it's not always bad. Meaningful repetition is different from drill. Practicing the same thing ad infinitum is tiring for the horse, but where does one draw the line? How much practice is too much? When practice is meaningful, the rider (or the horse) knows **why** she's doing the exercise.

> ★ **Try This**

In the example on page 155, did your horse's shoulder-in lack the 10-meter bend that you wanted? Ask yourself (and notice the use of sequential thinking), *Am I able to ride a reliable 10-meter circle?* If you can't maintain the bend on a circle, it's not going to be possible to retain the bend as you go straight in shoulder-in. A meaningful exercise has to include 10-meter circles.

161

part three / chapter 11
Use Your Whole Brain to Enhance
Growth for You and Your Horse

Exercise with Intent

1. At the letter of your choice, practice a 10-meter circle in walk twice.

2. Then go straight in shoulder-in, retaining the 10-meter bend in walk.

3. At the next letter, circle 10-meters and then shoulder-in again.

4. Try it in the other direction, too.

This kind of quiet work is meaningful because there's a reason behind it. You're trying to maintain a consistent 10-meter bend and retain it in shoulder-in. You can be sure that when you achieve it, the horse will be rewarded primarily because of the improved balance, and secondarily because you may pat him and tell him he's a genius. Then you can try it in trot, and that, too, will have meaning. It's the meaningfulness that makes repetition different from drill.

Olympic champion Hubertus Schmidt practices half-pass until it is very good. Then he stops and praises the horse. The practice was meaningful. He wasn't simply trying to do the movement, but rather he was trying to do it well—with the connection from the inside leg to the outside rein confirmed so the collection can become extraordinary. The achievement is meaningful when the horse understands what he's trying to achieve. He needs to get to the point that the horse thinks, *Oh! This is what we're doing today!* Horses love that feeling.

Kinesthetic Learning

When a rider is simply aware of the concept of muscle memory and open to it, it should boost her learning ability and make her practice meaningful. When she thinks, *I'm practicing this again and again so that my muscles can do it by heart,* this might just happen.

It's unreasonable to expect success without practice.

When muscle memory of horse and rider take over, movement becomes somewhat automatic. It goes from the conscious brain to the unconscious brain. Then you are mentally *free*. Both horses and riders experience kinesthetic learning. Be aware of it.

Mental Practice

Remember the value of mental practice and your ability to practice perfectly when you're practicing mentally. Perfect practice makes perfect. Also make your mental practice specific, involving as many of your senses as possible. For example, in the exercise on page 51, from an active, relaxed, but powerful working trot, your horse bends through the corner with precise 10-meter bend and develops shoulder-in. Your horse steps with confidence and clear rhythm. His shoulders lift and he feels elastic in your hand. His back is swinging. *Make it great.* Feel his hindquarters step under you and carry you. Listen to the rhythm. Look at his elegant forehand. Breathe. Use all your senses. It's all in your mind, but tomorrow your chances of getting the same result for real are greatly enhanced.

Likewise, at a show, you might take quiet time and visualize the course or the test directly before you need to perform. It is one of the best ways to enhance your performance.

Teachers Need to Repeat

Kyra Kyrklund knows about the psychology of education. She knows she will need to repeat her recommendations often, and she's okay with that. She says that if she were to lecture her students, she'd be lucky if they remember 25 percent of what she says—even with a visual handout. Maybe if there were a cartoon next to each principle, they would do a little better, but she is at peace with the fact that 75 percent of what she says goes out the window.

Now, if you audit a clinic, you not only hear but you also see the results, so retention rate typically increases to 50/50—the auditor retains 50 percent and forgets 50 percent. However, if the student *rides* in the clinic, that rider will not only hear and see but also feel kinesthetically, and in this case the rider may retain 75 percent and forget only 25 percent. As the number of senses involved increases, so does the level of absorption. Reviewing video feedback after the clinic increases the sensual learning experience even more. Those who teach know that much of what they say isn't heard. After all, it's also true that a student can only pay attention to one thing at a time, and paying attention to the horse should be a priority. So teachers need to repeat. A good teacher doesn't get frustrated by that. In fact, she might say to the student, "I know how hard this is, so I don't mind repeating myself."

On the other hand, to be a good learner, you might make it a practice to never make the

part three / chapter 11
Use Your Whole Brain to Enhance
Growth for You and Your Horse

instructor repeat himself. Lendon Gray says that when she was first learning, she challenged herself to never hear the same instruction twice. If the instructor said her leg was too far forward, she exaggerated and put it too far back. Her toes were too far out? She put them too far in.

Consistency and Persistence

Many years ago, as a student of German master Walter Christensen, I *thought* I had the same conscientious mindset as Lendon Gray. I really valued those lessons with Walter, and I was determined to never make him tell me the same thing twice. Then one day as I passed him, he said, "Long the leg." I shoved my legs down with determination, but the next time I passed him, he repeated the same thing, "Long the leg." I, of course, thought they were down as far as they could go, but I pushed them down farther and probably managed another half-inch. The third time he said, "Long the leg," I mentally protested, thinking that perhaps Walter was forgetting how short I am, but I shoved them down even more.

We discussed the principle of "grounding" back on p. 69—when the rider is grounded to the earth, the horse very easily goes in front of the leg. And that's what happened years ago. I pushed my legs down as far as they possibly could go, and the horse surged in front of my leg. Just as I was thinking, "Oh, wow!" there was a roar of approval from Walter—"*JA!*" The result in my horse's carriage was as visible to him as it was to me.

This was an easy fix. It just required persistence, but some corrections are much more difficult to make than others. For example, whereas it's fairly easy to fix the length of the rider's legs, it's more

*Great riders
are endlessly persistent
about the basics.*

difficult to fix a rider's essential leg position—for a variety of reasons. That requires more persistence. On the other hand, if your hands need to be lower, that should be easy to fix. Sometimes the elbows are stiff and sometimes the shoulders are too far back. Whichever is the cause, both instructor and student can expect to fix that quickly—unless, of course, you think the hands are high because of the hands. The hands can't lower themselves without cooperation from the elbows, shoulders, or sometimes the whole upper body if it's leaning back. This harkens back to the importance of *sequence* (see p. 150). The same is true of the need to lower your heels. This can't be done without help from the hips and knees, and it can't be done without relaxing the muscles on the top of the foot. Sequence!

When you practice, be sure you're as consistent as possible, giving the exact same aids and expecting the exact same desired result. That's the definition of a *consequent* trainer (see p. 29), and it requires concentration as well as physical skill.

Be persistent about the qualities you want. This persistence is the difference between good riders and great riders. Great riders are endlessly persistent about the basics.

*How Two Minds Meet:
The Mental Dynamics
of Dressage*

Practice and Repetition TIPS

✓ *Practice and repetition come naturally to people who are passionate about any pursuit. They never seem to tire of practicing because they regard it as fun rather than work. It is the repetitive nature of endless practice that creates geniuses in any field of endeavor.*

✓ *Repetition is how horses learn. They want to know the purpose of their exercises, and this becomes clear to them only with repetition. However, repetition can become drilling if the horse doesn't understand what he's doing or he becomes physically tired.*

✓ *Some riders stay in the Comfort Zone and avoid practicing skills that are difficult. Others like to tackle these same skills, and of course, this latter group of riders excel because they are willing to stretch in order to achieve.*

✓ *Riders and teachers should be aware of how the riding should feel. Awareness of kinesthetic learning and muscle memory can enhance learning. After all, it's impossible for the teacher to explain a feeling. Only the horse can teach how a 10-meter circle feels, how a half-pass feels, how the connection ideally feels.*

✓ *When you can't practice physically, you can practice mentally, and visualize your best performance. Top competitors visualize the ride before performance time.*

✓ *Good instructors understand the need to repeat. They know that riders need to listen to their horses as well as listening to them. They know how hard it is to break bad habits. They don't mind repeating—to a point. At some point, the rider needs to tell herself what to do and take responsibility for learning.*

✓ *Practice and repetition, over time, becomes persistence. Consistent persistency is a powerful way of learning. Good riders are endlessly persistent about the basics.*

part three / chapter 11
Use Your Whole Brain to Enhance
Growth for You and Your Horse

*How Two Minds Meet:
The Mental Dynamics
of Dressage*

{11.5} Ribbons can be shallow rewards, but they can also indicate that you and your training are on the right track.

4. The Principle of Reward

Conrad Schumacher says, "Good riding is the best reward for the horse." Likewise, the best reward for the rider is a great feeling. And that great feeling—that reward—comes as a result of practice.

Kyra Kyrklund is an expert on learning theory, and she is one who talks about the 10,000 repetitions it takes to learn a skill. After you do your 10,000th shoulder-in, it might be close to perfect. It might be excellent. How did it feel? Fabulous? This feeling is the greatest reward—for both horse and rider! But the first days of riding shoulder-in won't be so good, and riders have to push through that while making it as easy as possible for the horse. Schoolmasters help. When the horse knows more than the rider, he can give the rider the right feeling and a good instructor can help lead horse and rider to that place.

It's impossible to explain how a song sounds, a wine tastes, or how a horse should feel, but the teacher can set the horse and rider up for success, usually with sequential exercises that are likely to give the right result. Then at just the right moment, the instructor says, *"That's it! That's* what you want! Did you *feel* that?" The teacher informs and rewards the rider as the horse rewards the rider, and the rider rewards the horse—just as Walter Christensen did for me. Everyone gets a reward—even the instructor because it looks so beautiful! The horse's reward, like that of the rider, is the great feel of the energy going "through" his entire body, which is innately rewarding as he uses his whole self positively. Successful instructors are aware that when lessons leave both the student and the horse with the reward of a good feeling, those lessons are more likely to be remembered and those feelings

167

part three / chapter 11
Use Your Whole Brain to Enhance
Growth for You and Your Horse

are more likely to be repeated. Imagine, it's far more rewarding than if your instructor gave you a candy as you left.

Horse show ribbons are another form of shallow reward, except that they often have a much deeper meaning (11.5). Winning a ribbon might mean that you're on the right track! And if you're in good company, and you placed well within that stiff competition, it's even more assurance of the quality of your training. That thumbs-up from the judges is an important confidence boost! It's a green light to proceed, and the judge's comments might give details as to *how* the rider might proceed.

Sugar cubes and carrots as a reward for a horse's correct response to the rider's aids are useful if they're used with discernment. The rider can't be indiscriminate about when this delicious reward is dealt out. If the rider is *consequent*, the horse will understand the treat as a reward for a good performance. The greatest reward, however, is to go straight, out of the movement, and pat him on the neck after a good half-pass or pirouette.

Circus trainers are often phenomenal trainers because they are able to teach horses to perform on command by utilizing the principles of reward. Riders in other disciplines could utilize their techniques of teaching horses to understand. They are exceptionally effective at teaching concepts to horses, and when the horse understands, he's usually willing and able to perform regardless of whether traditional aids are used. However, when the traditional aids *are* used, the horse uses his body in the healthiest way. Dressage is the mental and physical training of horses for whatever

The best reward for the horse is good riding.

discipline. Mentally, we want our horses to understand and enjoy their work, developing confidence and trust along the way. Physically, we want them to develop their muscles in such a way that they carry themselves with efficiency, power, and comfort, minimizing the chance of injury.

Beware of the situation in which the perfectionist rider might subconsciously withhold rewards from her horse because she isn't satisfied. The armchair critic perched on her shoulder is relentlessly telling her that the work isn't good enough. Or sometimes there's a problem with a wringing tail or a busy stallion mouth or a tongue that the rider doesn't have direct control of, and it drives her nuts. Beware of those feelings of disappointment. Don't let the horse who is trying his heart out become discouraged or feel he isn't good enough. The very evolved rider can praise her horse even when she is dissatisfied or disappointed because she wants her horse to know that his performance is appreciated or that it's better, even if it's only a little better.

The other side of that coin is the naughty horse who actually doesn't deserve a reward. He might require a swift correction, a la herd mentality, a request for the right behavior, and then hopefully a prompt reward that is deserved. You need to be in a position in which the horse is rewarded more often than not.

The Passionate Student

As we know, some of us have an extreme passion for riding horses. Others have an unexplained need to swim or play golf, but those of you reading this book ride horses. It's fun, and it puts you into the flow of continuous motivation. It's in the blood, and the intensity of that innate need is the motivating force behind accelerated learning. It's not only the 10,000 repetitions that come so easily, but it's also the feelings behind each of those reps. In the case of equestrian sports, it's also love for horses and often one horse in particular.

Passion can take you a long way. Event rider Kim Walnes had a horse named The Gray Goose, and the two of them rose to fame in a few short years, winning an individual bronze medal at the World Championships in Luhmühlen in 1982. Kim had such fun as she devised challenges for her extraordinary horse. At one point, I remember her setting up a straight-backed chair in the field just so they could jump something fun and different. Her attitude was playful, passionate, and determined.

"I am a very ordinary person, who happens to have had a very powerful dream," said Kim.

No one could ever love a golf club or a basketball like we love horses. Horses are a unique and powerful force, and that passion affects the speed of learning tremendously. Sometimes just being in the saddle is our reward.

Reward TIPS

✓ *Reward will increase the likelihood of learning a certain behavior.*

✓ *The right feeling is the best reward for both horse and rider.*

✓ *Horse show ribbons might indicate that horse and rider are on the right path.*

✓ *Sugar cubes and peppermints are useful when used with discernment.*

✓ *The perfectionist rider might subconsciously withhold reward from a horse who is trying his best and performing well because of a bad habit (such as a wringing tail or a busy mouth) that annoys the rider.*

✓ *For the passionate rider, just being in the saddle is adequate reward.*

169

part three / chapter 11
Use Your Whole Brain to Enhance
Growth for You and Your Horse

5. The Principle of Primacy

That which you learned first, you learned best and you will remember best. This principle of *primacy* underscores the importance of learning correctly the first time. The process of unlearning and relearning after going down the wrong path is time consuming and emotionally trying. Remember what Malcolm Gladwell and Kyra Kyrklund said: it takes 10,000 repetitions to learn a skill. If you learned it wrong, it takes 5,000 repetitions to undo that habit and another 10,000 repetitions to learn it correctly. The road back is a long one.

When it comes to retraining horses, they have no moral code that says, *Wow, I need to change my ways.* If your horse learned incorrectly, you may not be able to reverse his original learned training. It's common and reasonable to think, *I know what's wrong, so I can fix it.* Not necessarily. On the other hand, when a horse was originally well trained and subsequently falls into less-than-skilled hands, that superior training usually shines through when a skilled rider returns to the saddle.

The trials of learning incorrectly apply not only to physical technique but also to mental attitude. When a rider learns from a teacher with a negative attitude, or she learns from a horse who required that she *make* him work because he was an unwilling participant, she has fallen into the category of learning wrong. It will require some relearning. Not only will the technique your horse learned first be difficult (sometimes impossible) to undo and redo, his attitude toward the training will be hard to change. This all points to the importance of doing things right the first time, which requires choosing the right instructor.

Students sometimes gravitate toward instructors who will let them compete at unrealistically high levels. Judges get frustrated when they see a nice rider who would get a high score if she were riding at the right level. So she gets a 60 percent at Fourth Level when she would have received a 74 percent at Second Level and a 69 at Third Level. The judge would much rather give high scores. Later, when this rider is back down at the level where she belongs, it's pretty tough on the ego, and she may even give up showing.

*We all tend to ride our horses
in the same way
we live our lives.*

Most instructors read from the same library of equestrian knowledge, but that doesn't directly translate into teaching the same, so students would do well to observe potential instructors to be sure they are teaching the basics, and also that their students reflect that basic knowledge.

Finding the right instructor is very personal not only because of the technical aspects, but also because of emotional aspects. Riders gravitate toward teachers who share the same values and philosophies of life. We all tend to ride our horses in the same way that we live our lives. It's ideal when that instructor is your first instructor.

First Things First

Competitive riders know the value of a first impression. In dressage, it's the entrance. That centerline is important, and competitive riders know to practice them. German master Johann Hinnemann asks his riders to finish every lesson with a centerline. That's not a bad idea because the centerline is difficult. When you enter with a bold but relaxed and straight entrance and land like a feather in a square halt exactly at X, this tells the judge a great deal

about the training. You don't do that by accident, and that first impression can arguably influence more than the first mark (fig. 11.6).

At the beginning of Lendon Gray's clinic lessons, she usually asks the student, "What's the thing you do best?" One of the most important aspects of learning is recognizing what is good (and recognizing it in the beginning), which increases the chances of that positive quality being retained while building on the next thing.

As a teacher, you would like your student to recognize, for example, that the rhythm is good, so you can acknowledge this and increase the chances of retaining that rhythm as the difficulty increases. After establishing the positive qualities and mentally confirming them, then it's the time for the instructor to ask, "What would you like to improve?" The answer reveals information about the student's understanding of sequence, and the instructor can agree with the student or say, "Great. Let's improve the canter first and *then* we'll work on the flying changes." You can't work successfully with flying changes until the canter is consistently working and balanced.

As you know, skills that the horse and rider learn out of sequence give the wrong feeling—to both horse and rider. The student could work on flying changes, but it would give the wrong feeling if the underlying basics aren't established. The horse needs to have a quality canter, he needs to be supple, straight, and in front of the leg. He needs to be engaged enough that he can do canter-walk-canter transitions, and balanced enough to do counter-canter. In addition, if these flying changes are the horse's first experience with them, they would be difficult to undo. First things first.

part three / chapter 11
Use Your Whole Brain to Enhance
Growth for You and Your Horse

{11.6} Courtney King Dye rides Idocus to a lovely square halt. Competitive riders know the value of a first impression. In dressage, it's the entrance.

Chapter One, Page One

Most riders are inclined to fall into an emotional and conceptual trap that goes like this: Annabel had a fabulous ride on Tuesday, so she can't wait for Wednesday when she assumes they will pick up where they left off. It seems a reasonable, logical conclusion that if she does A and B on Tuesday, she might look forward to C on Wednesday.

With horses, it doesn't always work like that. Any number of circumstances can fall into play. Maybe the horse will be tired on Wednesday because he worked so hard on Tuesday. Maybe the wind will be whipping at 40 miles an hour, and he'll be tense. Maybe Annabel won't ride as well because she's tired or sore. Wednesday might be a great day, but the chances are immensely improved if Annabel goes back to Chapter One, Page One at the beginning of Wednesday's ride.

The warm-up is to "warm up" the horse's muscles and re-engage his mind. He needs to be physically and mentally prepared for C on Wednesday. It might happen, but the chart of progress doesn't normally look like the Volvo slash. There are ups and downs—you hope with an overall upward tendency.

Regardless, when the rider returns to Chapter One, Page One in the warm-up each day, the primary skills (the basics), get confirmed and reconfirmed until it can be said, "That horse has great basics!" Fortunately, when you're reading books, you don't have to start at Chapter One, Page One every day. You can start today where you left off yesterday. That's not true of horses. Every day: Chapter One, Page One.

As your horse becomes more educated, he will spend less time on Chapter One, but you should always touch upon the "basics, " from which everything else is built. The Grand Prix horse, because of his physical development and mental culture, will begin his warm-up in a more balanced place, but the warm-up will be very much the same as that of a four- or five-year-old. You always start where the horse's natural balance is, then ask little questions. Can you bend left and right on a 20-meter circle? Can you turn left? Turn right? Can you stretch? Can you do this—and that?

173

part three / chapter 11
Use Your Whole Brain to Enhance
Growth for You and Your Horse

✓ That which you (and your horse) learned first, you and he will learn and remember best.

✓ Your horse has no inner moral code, so if he learned incorrectly to begin with, it may be difficult or impossible for him to unlearn and relearn to your liking.

✓ On the other hand, if a horse was well trained to begin with and falls into the hands of a poor rider, he can usually regain his former ways when a skilled rider returns to the saddle.

✓ If your first instructor is the right instructor who teaches the basics you are fortunate.

✓ In competition, the first impression is often a lasting one.

✓ At the beginning of your ride, it's important to acknowledge that which you and your horse do well so those skills are confirmed.

✓ The warm-up is a time for relaxation, confirming and reconfirming the basics.

6. The Principle of Recency

*R*ecency is the opposite of *primacy*. Instead of looking only at what you learned first, you also consider the most recent experience. All other things being equal, what you learned most recently, you remember better than what you learned last week, and what you learned last week, you remember better than what you learned last month. If you need to *apply* a skill soon after learning it, you will remember it better. If you are asked to do a shoulder-in, for example, and just moments ago, you *saw* an excellent execution of shoulder-in by a skilled rider in your barn, you have the advantage of seeing it recently, and you have the power of the Principle of Imitation working in your favor. If you saw that excellent shoulder-in a week ago or a month ago, your chances of imitating it accurately are reduced more and more as time goes on.

What are other practical applications of this principle of recency?

• *Teachers who recap and review the information conveyed in their lessons at the end of the lesson are more successful at fixing the lesson in the student's mind and body.* For example, "Your horse's rhythm improved throughout your ride, which proves that your work was correct. Next, we will work on adding power, especially in the lateral work, without losing the relaxation. Then the rhythm will improve even more."

• *Teachers can multiply the effectiveness of the recap.* Those who end their lessons on a positive note (The Principle of Reward, p. 167) and give the rider a sense of confidence (The Principle of Intensity, p. 177) are more likely to have their lessons remembered! For example, "If you're able to reproduce that last medium trot at the horse show next weekend, it could get a score of 8 or 9. You can do it!"

- ***Teachers who give their riders homework at the end of the lesson will have a high chance of making progress before their next lesson.*** The teacher might say, "If you practice exercises that combine lateral work and lengthened strides, the lateral work will become more powerful and the lengthenings will become more supple." (As an aside, the ability to conceive of the idea to combine powerful lengthenings with lateral work comes from how your left-brain information is organized in your mind (see p. 77). Regardless, the student who is given homework is motivated because she knows the positive result she can *expect* from doing this homework.

Whether you're an instructor or a student or both, pay attention to how the lesson ends.

The Primary and Recent Experiences of a Schoolmaster

Annabel is a First Level rider who purchased a Fourth Level schoolmaster named Mastery. For the first month, Mastery gave Annabel wonderful new feelings of uphill carriage and swing in the back, but then he started to carry himself poorly, and Annabel was incapable of doing even Second Level movements well. Mastery appeared to have lost his edge in only a month.

This happens often. We have to remember that every rider is a trainer. Every time Annabel got on Mastery, she was expecting to feel what she always used to feel—a First Level horse. That's human nature. Annabel also did what she always did to get a First Level performance. Annabel had lessons several times a week, which definitely helped her ride better and change her expectations, but a rider can't develop enough to become proficient at Fourth Level without spending time.

Mastery lowered himself to Annabel's level of expectation, which isn't a poor reflection on the horse. Horses don't plot to undo us. They

175

part three / chapter 11
Use Your Whole Brain to Enhance
Growth for You and Your Horse

Primacy and Recency

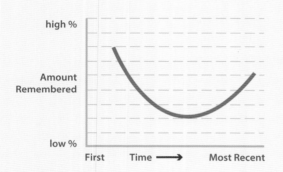

{11.7} The combined principles of primacy and recency show how we remember what we learn.

When you combine the principles of primacy and recency, you see a graph that's similar to a very flat U with the left side of the U slightly higher than the right side (fig. 11.7). This graph indicates that what you learned first, you remember best. Gradually the power of memory fades throughout the middle of the lesson (or the year or your lifetime), only to creep upward toward the end. That which you learn last is remembered second best. ●

Schoolmasters need to be refreshed by a rider who has the skills to help the horse's primary schooling resurface.

are simply in the moment and they do what they're told. Annabel's aids simply told him to do First Level. That said, horses with less-than-ideal character do take advantage of the rider who isn't a leader at Fourth Level ability, which is why the term "schoolmaster" is reserved for the horse who is on the rider's side.

All schoolmasters do need to be refreshed by a rider who not only has the skills to ride the higher level, but also *expects* the horse to carry himself as well as possible. Then, the schoolmaster's *primary* schooling usually resurfaces. Gradually (often very gradually), Annabel learns to expect more and she learns how to ask for more and ride that Fourth Level horse. At this point, Mastery's "recent experiences" will be more in line with his "primary experiences," and horse and rider will be "on the same page."

How Two Minds Meet:
The Mental Dynamics
of Dressage

✓ *All other things being equal, what you learned most recently will be learned and remembered second best—behind that which you learned first (primarily).*

✓ *The students of a teacher who recaps and reviews the content of their riding lesson at the end of it, will recall the lesson most clearly. If that review includes utilization of other Principles of Learning, the recap will be even more powerful.*

✓ *Teachers who give their riders homework will increase the success of the lesson.*

✓ *Schoolmasters bring their (primary) good training to the table for the student, and the student brings her less educated (recent) riding to the table. The schoolmaster needs regular lessons from a skilled rider to refresh his primary training in order to stay on track.*

● 7. The Principle of Intensity

There are actually very few "great teachers" in the world. They are rare. Those who are "great" add an energizing element of intensity to their lessons. They use humor, enthusiasm, demonstrations, analogies, examples, and they relate personal experiences. They invite the student to use as many senses as possible. Students see the horses become more beautiful, they hear the rhythm, and they imagine how it feels. The student is rapt. These great teachers don't just educate. They entertain, and the power behind their presentations give students confidence. The sheer energy put forth by great teachers is motivating and empowering to the students.

Caring and Greatness

Great Britain's Carl Hester is a *great* teacher because he has a massive amount of knowledge and he cares. He also has many of the positive traits I just mentioned. His students laugh, and in so doing, their minds open; they're in a frame of mind to retain his comments and his stories. Carl is a multiple-time Olympian, and he had countless relatable experiences on his path to those Games. Because he cares, he tells you about his experiences. He remembers when he was a young, struggling professional, and he tells you how he felt and what he did, for example, to acquire quality horses to ride. He tells you about his horses' daily schedules, how he keeps safety in mind first, what he finds when he teaches in different parts of the world. He says that he finds all the same problems such as helping riders learn

177

part three / chapter 11
Use Your Whole Brain to Enhance
Growth for You and Your Horse

how to make a downward transition in an upward manner (p. 58). He lets you know that you're not alone. "Riders all over the world have this problem," he says. He tells you how his horse Utopia had a very small walk and how he lost points for that. On and on, he cares and shares.

Finnish Olympian Kyra Kyrklund also lives in Great Britain, and she's a *great* teacher. She shares the qualities that make Carl Hester great. An auditor at one of her symposiums once asked if she should use the seat, legs, and hands all at the same time in a half-halt. Kyra promptly reached down and grabbed a clod of footing as if she were making a snowball and said, "You can't pack this footing into a ball without closing your fingers on all sides. It's the same with the horse. You can't close his frame without closing the aids from all sides."

She had instantly found an appropriate analogy that invited the students to use more than the sense of hearing. In her symposiums she often rode every horse at least once. She shared her experiences and made people laugh. She made people feel that they were not alone.

U.S. Olympian and former Dressage Team coach Robert Dover is a *great* teacher. He has the ability to simplify difficult concepts and make the rider feel she could be fabulous. Whereas he is honest, he also has an extraordinary ability to find the strengths of an individual and instill confidence while quietly working away on the weaknesses.

U.S. Olympian Lendon Gray is a *great* teacher. She founded Dressage4Kids, the organization within which she and others teach young riders all over the United States. Most of these young

> *Teachers who are 'great' add an energizing element of intensity to their lessons.*

riders probably don't even know that Lendon is an Olympian. They only know that she is their champion. She is the champion for every one of them. She learned dressage in the back woods of Maine, and she's in a good position to tell young riders how to excel without lots of help. She empowers them to take responsibility for their own learning. "Okay, now instead of me telling you, again and again, to look up, how about if you tell yourself to do it?" And as for the phrase, "Just do it," she said that long before it was the Nike slogan.

German trainer, Conrad Schumacher is a *great* trainer. He is a master of sequence (p. 150), which almost guarantees a student's improvement, and he brings deep caring and enthusiasm to his lessons.

There are other great teachers in the world, but greatness is rare. Fortunately there are many, many excellent riding teachers who enjoy local or regional fame, and the best ones always care deeply, they understand theory, and their students ride well.

Negative Intensity

Teachers who terrify their riders are working off the wrong kind of intensity. But it happens.

Some teachers ask their students to do things that might cause the horse to unseat the rider. Learning under fire doesn't work. Teachers who scream at their students are operating from a place of ignorance and frustration. They don't know the answers, so they become emotional and erode the confidence of their students.

Challenging the student is another matter. Learning, for horse and rider, happens outside of the Comfort Zone—in the Stretch Zone that might be in emotionally uncomfortable territory, but not in the Panic Zone (see p. 71). The experienced trainer and instructor knows how to play on the edge—challenging horse and rider without getting them too nervous or risking unsoundness in the horse. Students who have been challenged often come away finding that they can do more than they ever thought possible!

Personal Sound Systems

Personal sound systems revolutionized teaching by improving the quality of experience for everyone involved. The instructor can be easily heard over distance or over elements such as the wind. It's simply easier for the instructor to speak and for the student to hear. With the advent of personal sound systems, screaming was suddenly unnecessary. As a result, the tone of the lesson is inevitably nicer.

When the instructor can speak in normal conversational tones, it has an impact on the rider's frame of mind, and in turn, on how the horse receives the message.

The instructor can also convey more information when she can speak in conversational tones. She can explain the why and the when more easily if she doesn't need to shout and wonder if her words are being carried away by the wind. The student can say, "I don't understand," or "Wow, that feels better," or the teacher can say, "He looks lazy." And the student can reply, "Really? He feels like a firecracker." More information means both parties are better informed.

The better sound systems are two-way and give the instructor valuable feedback on the students' feelings, attitudes, and even on their physical well-being.

Health of the Rider

Occasionally, a rider has difficulty breathing. The instructor, through the sound system, can tell if the student is breathing through her mouth. Is the rider unfit? A skilled young rider went from Arizona to Connecticut, and the instructor noticed that she was out of breath while riding. Why? She was apparently allergic to something in Connecticut. She hadn't had trouble in Arizona, so this was brought to the attention of the rider and her parents, and they solved the problem. ▶

179 _____

part three / chapter 11
Use Your Whole Brain to Enhance
Growth for You and Your Horse

Personal Sound Systems

Attitude of the Rider

The rider's attitude is immediately evident through the sound system. Most riders talk to their horses. "What a good girl! Good job!" And when things go wrong, "Come on, you can do it. You're so brave!" It helps the horse tremendously to have a rider who's emotionally a team player. If the attitude has a hint of fear or impatience, the instructor knows that and can give suggestions and set some task-oriented goals that will help horse and rider feel successful and put the rider in the position of being the leader.

Feelings of the Rider

There are limitless examples of rider feedback, and the rider is, in fact, the only one on top, so her impressions can be very helpful to the training. "He feels a little tired today," can indicate the onset of the flu, a tick-borne disease, or a simple case of fatigue. "He feels a little wooden today," can mean the onset of a joint issue or soreness from the previous day's work. "Does the right hind look okay?" might cause you to pay special attention to that. "No, it doesn't look perfect, but I was wondering if it was my imagination." On the other hand, the rider might say, "It feels like I'm sitting on a bomb," when the horse can actually appear lazy. That information can govern the instructor's warm-up suggestions and help the horse become more supple and relaxed.

Receptiveness of the Rider

Sometimes the rider's brain is too busy, and she chats endlessly, thereby eliminating the possibility for conversation with the horse. (The same is true of some instructors who talk too much.) Feeling, by its nature is a receptive activity, but many riders are in a different mode much of the time. Developing feeling requires listening to the horse. It requires a lot of listening, and some riders don't know how to do that.

Many riders, for example, know academically speaking that the trot has two beats, the walk has four beats, and the canter has three beats with a moment of suspension. However, they can't really feel it, and as a result, they can't accurately half-halt because they don't understand the timing of the aids. The rider must know when the right hind, for example, is pushing off, when it is reaching forward, and when it is flat on the ground and engaged. If the rider can't feel this, she can't influence the horse at the right time. There's only one moment when she can effectively drive: when the horse's joints are bent and he's about to push off. There's only one moment when she can effectively influence the direction of the leg: when the hind leg is reaching. There's only one

How Two Minds Meet:
The Mental Dynamics
of Dressage

moment when she can add weight to a hind leg: when the hind leg is flat on the ground. With the personal sound system, the instructor can assist with tiny details, such as helping the student find these moments. The rider must be able to feel, and in order to feel, she has to concentrate and be open to listening to the movement of her horse. For every tick there has to be a tock. Speak-listen-speak-listen. For every effective conversation, there has to be input and output. The rhythm of the horse's gaits naturally provides the medium for this give and take. Riders need to silence the busy brain and listen.

With the personal sound system, the instructor not only can give suggestions easily but be receptive to her student. Then they can discuss training plans as quietly as if they were sitting over a cup of coffee. It's a joy. ●

Intensity TIPS

✓ *Great teachers bring an energizing intensity to their lessons, as well as humor, enthusiasm, and caring. They share by relating their own experiences and telling stories that motivate and empower their students.*

✓ *There are many excellent teachers who care deeply, understand theory, and teach their students to ride well.*

✓ *Negative intensity such as anger and impatience has no role in training horses.*

✓ *Personal sound systems allow the teacher and student to communicate in much greater depth.*

part three / chapter 11
Use Your Whole Brain to Enhance
Growth for You and Your Horse

● 8. The Principle of Accountability

Studies have shown that students who will be tested learn better than those who will not be tested. In addition, those who are quizzed do better when they know there is a final exam. They know they can't forget the answers after the quiz. The questions will reappear in the future.

In equestrian sport, this principle translates to mean that those who compete at horse shows learn better than those who do not go to horse shows. Those who go to local shows do better if they plan to finish the season at a regional championship. Accountability *can* be about anxiety. At a show, the rider is often out of the Comfort Zone, exposing herself to countless variables: shipping to the show, stabling that might be cramped and inconvenient, the physical stress of moving equipment to the stabling, setting up a space for tack and for feed. The weather is blustery, the horse is nervous, he doesn't like his new neighbor. The footing is different, and in places it's slippery. And so on.

What kind of rider are you? Do you find this situation exciting? You can't wait to overcome all these obstacles, and it's easy to see beyond them? Or, does this intimidate the heck out of you?

Now, what kind of horse do you have? Does he welcome the challenges and find this interesting and fun? Or, does it intimidate the heck out of him?

Weigh these situations, and be sure you're prepared. If you're confident, you can probably handle your intimidated horse, and vice versa. He'll manage under your supervision. If you're intimidated, you can probably manage with a confident horse, but not a fearful one.

Looking at your combined situation, are you edging into the Stretch Zone or are you solidly in the Stretch Zone and edging into the Panic Zone (see p. 71)? Are you and your horse both challenged? Acknowledge the factors that are out of your control, and manage the controllable ones:

• Can you bring a helper?

• Do you have a coach who will help you and your horse relax and feel confident?

Many riders don't know what they want. They don't ride with an immediate goal.

- Be sure you're ultra-prepared in the skill department by showing at a level that's very comfortable for your horse.

The idea of presenting challenges and being accountable only works for you if you're ultimately successful—however you define that. For some, success might be a 65 percent, for others a 75 percent, but it shouldn't be about survival, and it shouldn't be about whether or not your horse will canter or stay in the ring.

Goals can fall into immediate, short-, or long-term categories. In the sidebar on page 184, you'll read about Reiner Klimke's amazing long-term goal, which was at least a two-year goal. It could have been longer. An immediate goal is one that you want to achieve today—for example, you want to improve your horse's bend on the circle. That doesn't take long. You're patient, but improvement can happen within a few minutes. That circle doesn't need to be perfect. Your goal is to make it better.

It's important that you understand timelines. Achieving correct flexion should not take days. Improving the bend should not take weeks. With help, these can be achieved in a day. Perfecting

a flying change will probably take at least a year. With the help of your trainer, set realistic goals for you and your horse.

Riding with Immediate Goals

Many riders don't know what they want. They don't ride with an immediate goal. It's as if they were walking around the house looking for something. A helpful friend asks, "What are you looking for?" The answer, "I don't know. I'm just looking for something." That's exactly what many people do when they're riding.

If they were searching in the house and said, "I'm looking for my keys," they would have a much better chance of success.

Say to yourself, "What do I want? What am I looking for?"

Discover what you want. Then figure out the aids for what you want.

For example:

- "I want to bend my horse on this circle! " Okay!
- "I want my horse to be better balanced." Okay!

Know what you want and learn how to achieve it.

Riding with Short-Term Goals

In order to achieve your long-term goals, you need to have achievable short-term goals. For example, Dr. Klimke wanted to improve his seat so he had frequent longe lessons leading up to his ride at the 1984 Olympic Games where he won the individual gold medal. He was after the truth.

183

part three / chapter 11
Use Your Whole Brain to Enhance
Growth for You and Your Horse

Klimke's Amazing Long-Term Goal

It was 1982. Keep that in mind. My husband Alan and I went to Lausanne, Switzerland, to see the World Championships (forerunner of the World Equestrian Games). In those days, it was fairly uncommon for Americans to venture over the pond to watch dressage. We were overwhelmed with the victory of the late Dr. Reiner Klimke with his fabulous Hanoverian gelding Ahlerich. We had occasion to tell him so, and he was grateful. He and his wife, Ruth, invited us to their stable and their home in Münster, Germany, the following week. At the Münster Riding Club, we watched him ride several young horses and then went to their home, the walls of which were lined with glass cabinets filled with memorabilia and trophies. It was a museum of German dressage history, but curiously, there was an empty place in the center of the main cabinet that caught my husband's eye. He pointed to this blank area that was lit with a small spotlight.

"What is this empty place for?" he asked.

"That," said Dr. Klimke, "is the place where I will put the 1984 individual Olympic gold medal when I win it in Los Angeles."

Commitment. Focus. Goal-setting. Klimke had it all, and in 1984 he did, in fact, win that individual Olympic gold! We could just imagine it in the glass cabinet.

Many years later, I returned to Münster as the chaperone for four young riders who had won a trip to Europe through The Dressage Foundation. Ingrid Klimke, daughter of the late Dr. Klimke, was on our itinerary. After we watched Ingrid ride, we went to lunch with her, and I told her this story. She said, "I didn't know that, but it sounds just like my father."

Then Ingrid made a quiet phone call to her mother, Ruth, who invited the young riders to that very same home where the history of German dressage lined the walls in glass cabinets. Every young rider held that 1984 Olympic individual gold medal, and they considered it the emotional high point of their trip to Europe. ●

All great riders are in love with the truth. They're not interested in fooling anyone. They want to know what can be better so they can improve it.

★ **Try This**

Your long-term goal might be to compete at Second Level. You can reasonably do that next year if your First Level performances are good this year. Then you aim to:

- Master the shoulder-in.

- Evolve your lengthenings into mediums with more lift and an uphill tendency.

- Improve your horse's straightness, bending, suppleness, throughness, balance, and self-carriage.

- Improve his degree of collection by developing the weight-bearing ability of his hindquarters.

Then you have subsidiary goals. For example, in order for a lengthening to become a medium, it will need power and lift, so you can combine lengthening with your shoulder-in. You can also include a step or two of rein-back because that will help engage him and improve the collection.

Exercise to Build First Level Skills to Second Level

1. Start tracking right in trot from C (fig. 11.8).

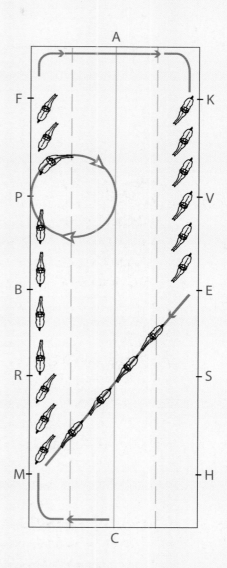

{11.8} Exercise to Build First Level Skills to Second Level

185

part three / chapter 11
Use Your Whole Brain to Enhance
Growth for You and Your Horse

2. From M to R, shoulder-in right.

3. From R to P, lengthen the stride.

4. At P, circle 10 meters.

5. From P to F, shoulder-in right.

6. At A, halt and rein-back one or two steps. Proceed in trot.

7. K to E, shoulder-in; and E to M, lengthen the stride on this short diagonal.

8. At C, circle left 20 meters in rising trot, allowing the horse to stretch (not shown).

9. Repeat in the other direction.

What will happen? Even if your execution isn't very good, the shoulder-in will add a bit of collection and lift to the lengthening, the 10-meter circles will help the shoulder-in, the lengthening will add power, the rein-back will improve engagement and collection, the stretchy circle will add throughness, and so on. Each small part of the exercise will add another layer of quality. Your lengthening will become a medium with time, and the other qualities you need will improve.

These are just small examples of how you can be smart about utilizing your riding time wisely. Don't wander around and hope you get better. Make a plan with reasonable goals and expectations.

Don't wander around and hope you get better. Make a plan with reasonable goals and expectations.

Dressage vs. Jumping

It's especially important that the dressage rider ride with a goal-oriented mindset because there are no innate motivations for the dressage horse to carry himself beautifully on that line from M to K, or any other line. The jumping horse has a "leg up" in this regard, because he can see his goal in the form of an obstacle, and he usually feels motivated to achieve. The rider of a jumping horse can feel the magnetic appeal of each fence in his hand and hence through his whole body. There's a party around every bend. For dressage horses, the party is perpetually postponed.

Dressage goals and destination points do, in fact, exist, but they are invisible to the horse. Fortunately, experienced dressage riders rise to the occasion by being actually excited about riding a specific line between two random points eagerly and precisely, but the horse doesn't always share the enthusiasm initially. The rider keeps encouraging him to respond to his invitation to the party, but of course, the horse must wonder, *Why should I do this?* It's important to acknowledge that the horse probably is wondering, *What's the point?* In

the meanwhile, for hunters, jumpers, and Western horses, there is actually a party going on that materializes in the form of a series of obstacles or tasks.

Dressage and flat work are more like the addictive human pursuits of Pilates and yoga—a gym with no machines. The successful dressage rider's enthusiasm for the non-existent party is contagious. After the working dressage horse starts to feel better and understand his gymnastic challenges, he becomes a dressage addict, too. He can't get enough of it. He feels freer in the front and becomes more and more self-motivated.

As the horse's training progresses and his work becomes harder, it is the rider's job to help maintain that addiction to his "gym" and eagerness to do the work. The rider challenges the horse so he improves, but she is sensitive enough to know when to rest or stop before her horse becomes too tired or frustrated. Even a horse who is 100 percent trained never loses the natural instinct to do his work in the easiest way, which would invariably mean he falls off the line of travel or loses the bend, which makes him less athletic. Without the help of the rider, he would lose his balance. The rider needs to maintain control. That means concentration on the immediate goal—which will bring you closer to the short-term goal and also closer to the long-term goal.

What's the Point?

Some teachers ask their students to fill out annual paperwork that describes their goals in detail so the teacher can tailor her teaching to the rider's needs. The instructor wants to know *how* each student will be accountable, and it depends on their goals.

187

part three / chapter 11
Use Your Whole Brain to Enhance
Growth for You and Your Horse

When the instructor teaches a lawyer, doctor, secretary, nurse, teacher, banker—anyone who works hard at another job all day, the instructor needs to know their goals. Many of these riders take their training very seriously and aspire to be as good as a professional. They spend their precious free time maximizing their ability to ride, and the teacher does well to help them maximize this. However, there is the strong possibility that the rider just needs to get some mental relaxation and some physical exercise. The teacher needs to know what the rider needs, and that might change from day to day. The rider might be especially tired on some days and just need to wind down and enjoy time with the horse. One way or the other, the warm-up for this rider isn't only a warm-up for the horse, but for the rider as well.

When the instructor teaches amateurs who are used to using their mental powers at work, they might think, *I'm trying!* In fact, they *are* trying, but they are trying more mentally than physically. The instructor needs to explain that to them. Horses require physical aids.

When teaching professional riders, the instructor can usually be tougher. The rider doesn't mind too much if she doesn't like the message, because she knows she must understand the truth. These professionals in training don't need to be entertained so the teaching style is often more direct.

When an instructor teaches children she needs to realize that they might be tired after school. They might have other problems, and maybe they need to play. The horse might enjoy this attitude, but he will teach the young rider about patience, and help her learn how to communicate. It's especially important that they teach with kindness and sometimes humor, but that doesn't mean that the training is less *consequent*. In Europe where riding clubs abound, even an eight-year-old learns that when you apply the aids, something must happen! There must be a consequence to the aids.

There are many styles of teaching that experienced teachers can implement unconsciously depending on their students' needs. Some riders need enthusiasm, others need laid-back assurance, others need analytical theory, and still others need the touchy-feely approach. There is literally no end to the styles that come as a package deal along with the basic knowledge and riding ability that should come with every instructor.

✓ *Studies show that students who are held accountable learn and retain knowledge better. In equestrian sport, this means that riders who go to horse shows and ride "tests" improve more than those who do not. Showing takes riders out of their Comfort Zone and into the more challenging Stretch Zone.*

✓ *Accountability means having goals: immediate goals (What do I want to achieve in the next 5 to 45 minutes?), short-term goals (What do I want to achieve this month?), and long-term goals (What do I want to achieve this year?).*

✓ *Dressage riders need to be attentive to making the ride interesting because unlike jumping horses, the obstacles are invisible. Dressage is more like the practice of yoga.*

✓ *Instructors need to learn their students' goals so they can tailor their teaching to meet the rider's needs.*

● 9. The Principle of Organization

Things learned in isolation are difficult to retain. For example, here are five words: horse, mirror, clock, knife, apple. If you were asked to repeat these words five minutes from now, you might remember "horse," but you might forget the rest unless you created meaning. Perhaps you imagined looking in the mirror and seeing an apple-shaped clock with a knife for the minute hand. You might remember these words because you've put them in some context and given them meaning, albeit ridiculous meaning.

We learn most easily by searching for information that will have meaning to us—maybe even important or urgent meaning. We want to know if a given piece of information can help solve a problem or give us a more sophisticated view of a challenging situation—like riding horses.

There is a system underlying all equestrian knowledge. Xenophon, born in 431 B.C., wrote not only about the thoughts of Socrates, but also *On Horsemanship.* Centuries of great horsemen have added to that base of knowledge. We do well to learn as much as we can from those who came before us because it's futile to reinvent this particular wheel.

As we continue to learn, we retain that which fits into the construct of our current knowledge. We each create our own little worlds of belief, based on the widely accepted huge bank of knowledge "out there" that is basically agreed upon. We organize it in the way that makes the most sense to us based on our previous knowledge and our previous attitudes. Our realities are molded by not only our own accumulated knowledge but by the opinions and ideas of our families, teachers, mentors, and peers. We look

189

part three / chapter 11
Use Your Whole Brain to Enhance
Growth for You and Your Horse

for patterns, as if we were doing a jigsaw puzzle—first with the edge pieces, we seek the boundaries and construct within it, adding to the meaning.

We're all subject to our own little interpretations of this knowledge, and in fact, the methods with which educated people currently train horses are wildly different. Trainers presumably learned the same essential body of knowledge and presumably teach the same body of technical knowledge. And if all these trainers were to take a test, they might all pass and generally agree.

However, you might think that would translate into a common system of riding and teaching, but it most assuredly does not. When it comes to sitting on a horse and telling others how to sit on a horse, it's hard to imagine these people are all reading the same book. We all pretty much agree on the basic knowledge, but the interpretation of it is quite varied, and the manner in which each teacher conveys the lesson can be wildly different because each teacher has her own system of organizing knowledge.

But, ideally, each interpretation should reflect the basic tenets of dressage: the Training Scale, the Purposes of the Tests (see Appendices, p. 206), the basics of a good riding position, the basics of how horses use their bodies, and how transitions and halt-halts should influence the horse.

Aside from the necessary equestrian knowledge, some instructors are better than others at teaching. The best ones incorporate a lesson plan.

A Lesson Plan

A lesson plan is a construct—an organizational plan—that contains the instructor's knowledge. The plan has a beginning, middle, and end, and

When you have a task, your success is measured by something concrete.

it has a timeframe. The term "lesson plan" may spark anxiety in the heart of seasoned instructors, or maybe boredom or frustration in the hearts of others, but the lesson plan simplifies everything. Whether you're an instructor with students or a rider who is the instructor for your horse, make friends with the lesson plan and it will become a part of you. It's not rocket science. The most basic lesson plan simply organizes the content of your lesson. It provides structure and clarifies how you're going to present your content. It prevents the potentially endless stream of content from taking over. Within the lesson plan, the content changes but the structure is disarmingly simple, and it's this very simplicity that makes the content so digestible.

A Task-Oriented Plan

When you have a task, your success is measured by something concrete ("How was my 15-meter circle?") rather than the general question of who has the upper hand in the possibly not-so-pretty dance. When you're the instructor, give your students tasks. When you're the rider, remember

WHAT TO DO
– A Suitable Five-Segmented Structure for a Lesson Plan –

1. **First 10 minutes:** *Walk. This important phase of the ride prevents injury by warming the horse's muscles, giving the joints time to loosen and allowing synovial fluid to flow. That's the physical part, but the mental part is equally important. Once the horse learns that he always has this relaxing walk, he comes to expect it, and the relaxation bleeds into the work phase. When the work phase becomes tense, the rider can return to the walk—even if only for a moment—and immediately regain his high quality of movement. The walk should become very good. This first 10-minute part of the ride can and should entail walk "work." The experienced rider accomplishes a lot during this session. The rider can practice transitions—for example, medium walk to free walk and back to medium walk. The rider can practice steering in the free walk with minimal use of the reins, and the horse is reminded to follow the rider's seat, leg, and weight aids. Toward the end of the walk work, the horse can do movements such as leg-yield in walk. This will improve the connection before the horse has even picked up trot and canter.*

2. **Next 10 minutes:** *Warm up in trot and canter. Regardless of your horse's level, you might concentrate on the first three qualities of the Training Scale. These, again, are the "basics." Concentrate on the rhythm of your horse's gaits. Ride forward in a clear and steady rhythm. Ride accurate 20-meter circles in both directions to develop suppleness and a correct connection. Work on developing good transitions between walk, trot, and canter to the right and to the left. The success of your half-halts won't be better than your transitions, so work on them until they're smooth and clear. Walk-trot-walk. Trot-canter-trot. Take a walk break somewhere within this 10-minute session. Be sure that your walk is correct.*

3. **Assessment:** *Walk at the end of the second 10-minute warm-up and assess. What aspects of your ride were good and what aspects need to be better? The content of the rest of your ride will be determined by your assessment of what quality or movement you would like to improve.*

191

part three / chapter 11
Use Your Whole Brain to Enhance
Growth for You and Your Horse

4. **Exercises 1, 2, and 3 (approximately 20 minutes total):** *Based on your assessment, decide on two or three exercises that will help your horse's weaknesses while still incorporating his strengths. Based on how your horse warmed up, your exercises might confirm what he already knows or they might introduce something new. Your plan needs to stay flexible, but know why these exercises will help. Know how and when to do them. If you're the instructor, explain it to your student. If you're the rider, explain it to your horse with your aids.*

5. **Cool down and walk (Approximately 5–10 minutes):** *Trot rising on a 20-meter circle. If you had a positive ride, he will be able to stretch, retaining the contact with fluidity. Let him walk and praise him.*

These five segments apply to a normal day in the life of training each horse. ●

that horses are herd animals: your horse wants and needs a leader, and you are the leader. When you give your horse a specific task, by definition, you are the leader of the dance. You're saying, "Let's do this 15-meter circle. Great. Now let's change direction and repeat that. Great." Next, do another task or exercise, and the dance will become much nicer as your horse starts to follow you.

A Positive Plan

Positive aids tell your horse what *to* do. Negative aids tell him what *not* to do. As you know, horses don't understand negative thoughts or ideas. If you, even subconsciously, tell your horse, "Don't spook at the flower box," he might actually perceive your message as: "Spook at the flower box." Instead, think of what you *do* want. You want him to flex in the direction opposite the flower box. You want an obedient, supple horse who is paying attention to you. You want to find uncluttered, sequential thoughts and clear aids for that task-oriented plan that usually develops an obedient and supple horse. You know your horse better than anyone. What helps him? What exercises will give him confidence and succeed in making him supple and put him in front of the leg?

The content of your step-by-step, positive, task-oriented lesson plan should be based on the guidelines provided by the Training Scale, by the dressage tests, and by the vast amount of equestrian knowledge of horsemanship, equine health, and technique. In the end, trainers who follow these guidelines should all be on the same page with regard to how to train horses in the safest, friendliest way so our equine friends love nothing more than being our partners.

How Two Minds Meet:
The Mental Dynamics
of Dressage

Organized Knowledge TIPS

✓ Organized material is stored in the context of other related material and is more likely to be remembered than random information.

✓ There is a time-honored system behind training horses that began centuries ago. Today's competition requirements reflect the theory and the knowledge of these great horsemen.

✓ Although the basic theory of training horses is well known, individual interpretation of that knowledge is varied.

✓ Teachers (and riders) should utilize the structure of a basic lesson plan.

✓ When problems arise, riders should use a task-oriented system of riding.

✓ The systems of schooling horses should be positive. Telling the horse what to do in a sequential way makes the job easy and understandable for the horse.

193

part three / chapter 11
Use Your Whole Brain to Enhance
Growth for You and Your Horse

CONCLUSION

How Two Minds Meet:
The Mental Dynamics
of Dressage

The *Probability* of Magic

Horses invite us to maximize the use of our thinking minds so we can be better horsemen and better riders. They require that we use our bodies as well as possible and utilize the classical technique that is described in *When Two Spines Align*. But more to the point, they persistently require that we explore other dimensions of the mind in search of the place where our two minds meet. Those other dimensions of the mind tap into a kind of magic that brings horse and rider to the threshold of the world of art—a place where the true beauty and spirit of the horse emerge.

It is there where we also find our higher selves, because that is what the horse requires. He asks us to be clear and positive and kind. The horse's persistent lesson is to help the rider leave her ego at the door and come to every day with love and compassion, a positive attitude, gratitude, and an openness to the probability of magic.

Categories of Knowledge

R andom knowledge only becomes useful when it is categorized and seen in the context of a larger picture. The forest is better understood when you can see and explore each tree within it. Information about training horses can be categorized. Learn about these topics, but also feel for them. Use your entire brain—left and right.

Here are the two most important categories of knowledge that instructors should teach and riders should learn:

- The Training Scale (or the Pyramid of Training)
- Purposes of the Dressage Tests

● The Training Scale

The time-tested Training Scale or Pyramid of Training provides arguably the best left-brained checklist ever created for training horses of all disciplines. It provides an organized sequence of qualities for the rider to monitor and regulate. But implementing this Training Scale is a whole-brained process. The rider can use as many senses as possible to explore every quality, and the result of training with this tool is the purpose of dressage: To strengthen and supple the horse while maintaining his calm and attentive demeanor. Here's how the Training Scale works:

COLLECTION
(Balance and Lightness of the Forehand from Increased Engagement)

STRAIGHTNESS
(Improved Alignment and Equal Lateral Suppleness on Both Reins)

IMPULSION
(Engagement and the Desire to Go Forward)

CONTACT
(Connection and Acceptance of the Bit through Acceptance of the Aids)

SUPPLENESS
(Elasticity and Freedom from Anxiety)

RHYTHM
(Regularity and Tempo)

"PHYSICAL DEVELOPMENT THROUGH PROGRESSIVE CONDITIONING"

"INCREASING THROUGHNESS AND OBEDIENCE"

USDF DEFINITION:
★ *Rhythm (Regularity and Tempo)*

The characteristic sequence of footfall and timing of a pure walk, a pure trot, and a pure canter. The rhythm should be expressed with energy and in a suitable and consistent tempo with the horse remaining in balance and self-carriage appropriate to its level of training.

Rhythm *(Regularity and Tempo)*

Our primary common language with the horse is tactile, and his primary contribution to the language is the rhythm of his gaits. We learn about it, but we also feel it and hear it. He has the four-beat walk with no period of suspension because he always has a foot on the ground; he has the evenly spaced two-beat trot with a period of suspension; and he has the three-beat canter, followed by a period of suspension.

Loss of rhythm or a disturbance in the pattern of the footfall is often caused by tension in the horse's back. You can feel that when it happens. Sometimes the walk is restricted too much by the rider, which results in the steps no longer being evenly spaced. Cavalletti and hill work improve the gaits, as does free walk on a long rein, but the greatest positive influence is a well-balanced rider who gives the aids at the right time—in the rhythm of the gaits. The working gaits are relaxed but active and the horse's back swings in rhythm, making it easy to give the aids in the right rhythm. The rider must feel for it rather than try to intellectualize it.

"Tempo" is the speed of the rhythm. The working gaits need to be in the most advantageous tempo. If the tempo is too fast, the horse will be inclined to get tense, which as you know, can cause rhythm issues. If it's too slow, he might become disconnected, which also can lead to rhythm issues. He might leave the hind legs on the ground too long and become strung out.

The ideal tempo is workmanlike, but there's a moment of relaxation within every stride. That is, it is self-perpetuating and consistent—like a human athlete pumping iron: flex-relax-flex-relax. That moment of relaxation is the reason why well-trained dressage horses often live long, useful lives.

When the horse changes the tempo without direction from his rider, he inevitably has lost his balance, his engagement, and his connection. Some horses are inclined to speed up and others slow down. Their normal inclinations are to speed up on straight lines and slow down on bent lines. Riders need to be aware of the tempo and monitor it by feel and by sound.

In competition, the gaits are judged on "freedom and regularity." Not only should the rhythm and tempo of the gaits be regular, but the skillful rider should allow her horse the maximum amount of freedom within the balance. As you know, that's what makes horses look beautiful and feel happy. Making the horse's gaits more beautiful and expressive is one of the primary objectives of dressage. Through the horse's years, the rhythm of the gaits ideally becomes more defined and cadenced. Be aware of the rhythm and tempo at all times. Feel for it. Listen for it. When the work is correct, the rhythm automatically improves. It's a reliable barometer for progress.

Suppleness *(Elasticity and Freedom from Anxiety)*

The purpose of the warm-up is to loosen the horse's muscles, relax him, and develop suppleness. Relaxation is a prerequisite to suppleness. If the horse isn't relaxed in

USDF DEFINITION:
★ *Suppleness* *(Elasticity and Freedom from Anxiety)*

Suppleness indicates the absence of negative muscular tension, allowing the joints to move with harmonious flexibility. Elasticity describes the horse that is able to stretch and contract the musculature smoothly and fluently.

Relaxation can refer to the horse's mental/emotional state (calm, without anxiety or nervousness) or the horse's physical state (to indicate the absence of muscular contraction other than that needed for optimal carriage, strength, and range and fluency of movement).

Usually the physical and the mental/emotional states go hand in hand.

the warm-up, he will never be relaxed when the work becomes more difficult, and he can't be supple, so be sure that you achieve this important goal. Signs of relaxation are a quiet, chewing mouth and a swinging tail that is a reflection of his relaxed, swinging back.

Conrad Schumacher uses the term "inner tranquility," which implies the horse's peaceful acceptance of the training and willingness to work with his rider. The search for inner tranquility is a wonderful one.

All horses, however, do get tense for a variety of reasons. Maybe your horse is naturally high strung, maybe he gets tense when the workload increases, maybe he's saying, "This is really hard for me," or "I don't understand what you want," or "The applause terrifies me," or "What's with the weird flower box?" Tension can never be avoided completely. The rider who never takes her horse out of the Comfort Zone will never progress, but a wise rider knows how to challenge her horse and bring him back to the Comfort Zone to regain relaxation, suppleness, and confidence. If you've established relaxation and suppleness to begin with, it usually only takes a few moments to regain it if the horse gets tense during the work session.

Horses often lose relaxation when they become more powerful. That might be when you ask for a lengthened stride, or it might be when he takes over and becomes more powerful on his own. Some degree of power is necessary in an elastic, supple horse, so it is important that your horse learns to stay relaxed as the power increases. It usually takes time.

When a horse loses relaxation, he typically stiffens by taking away the bend (lateral suppleness) and by flattening (longitudinal suppleness). Figures with bend—circles, corners, figure eights, and serpentines—help horses

How Two Minds Meet: The Mental Dynamics of Dressage

relax and regain suppleness, as do exercises such as leg-yield, shoulder-fore, shoulder-in, renvers, and half-pass. Stretching and transitions within and between gaits also help, and effective half-halts allow all these exercises to happen with maximum ease.

Be aware of the degree of relaxation and suppleness you have at all times. Teach your horse that he can increase power and stay relaxed. Exercises like the one on page 185 asks for shoulder-in, lengthening, and shoulder-in again. It teaches him that he can retain his suppleness when he adds power, and that he can regain his suppleness if he loses it. Soon, he will be more supple in the powerful work and more powerful in the suppling work. Again, whereas you monitor this quality with your left brain, you must feel it and listen for it when you work your horse. The suppleness will be reflected in his rhythmic breathing and the swing of his back.

Contact *(Connection and Acceptance of the Bit through Acceptance of the Aids)*

The rider cannot truly use her hands effectively until the horse draws on the rein—until he reaches through his topline and accepts contact with the bit as a result of the rider's driving aids. Elasticity in the connection is caused by the horse's correct response to his rider's driving aids. Energy from the hindquarters should go through the horse's body and cause the horse to reach for the bit. Ask yourself if your horse responds correctly to your driving aids. Feel for it. Elasticity cannot exist without this forward thrust and reach for the bit, and the rider can't truly use her hands effectively until the horse draws on the rein with honesty.

The quality of the contact has much to do with the sophistication of the rider's hands. The hand should be soft yet

USDF DEFINITION:
★ *Contact (Connection and Acceptance of the Bit through Acceptance of the Aids)*

The energy generated in the hindquarters by the driving aids must flow through the whole body of the horse and is received in the rider's hands. The contact to the bit must be elastic and adjustable, creating fluent interaction between horse and rider with appropriate changes in the horse's outline. Connection is the state in which there is no blockage, break, or slack in the circuit that joins horse and rider into a single, harmonious, elastic unit. It is a prerequisite for "throughness" (see p. 205).

201

solid. If the hands are too soft or unsteady, the horse doesn't have a bit he can commit to. And if the rider's hands are too hard (with tight fists), then the horse won't want to reach toward a bit that feels unfriendly. It's not always the rider's fault. It's impossible to have good hands until the seat is flexible and independent, and that takes time. Longe lessons are the best way to achieve the independent seat and good hands. Then, with experience, good hands become educated hands.

Horses are inclined to use one side of the body differently from the other. Like people, they are either stronger on the left or the right. When a horse is unequal in the hand, it is safe to assume he is not using his hind legs equally. Horses who aren't straight and even in the contact can show the common problem of tilting. Make sure that your horse's ears are level. Figure eights and serpentines are two of the best exercises to develop equal contact because they alternate between developing the connection from the inside leg to the outside rein going to the left and then going to the right. The horse usually becomes very straight and even in the hand.

It might be noted, that when you have the first elements of the Training Scale—Rhythm and Suppleness—your ability to have honest Contact (the third element) is easy. The stage is set. So if you have a problem such as uneven contact, go back to your suppling exercises and notice that it is more difficult to circle to one direction or the other. Work on that. Regaining the suppleness usually solves the problem. When the horse accepts the seat and leg aids, he isn't too reliant on the rein aids and he generally accepts the bit. He chews in a relaxed way, salivates, and has a wet, sometimes foamy mouth. This quiet, chewing mouth is also generally a reflection of a supple, swinging back.

USDF DEFINITION:
★ *Impulsion* (*Engagement and the Desire to Go Forward*)

Used to describe the transmission of an eager and energetic yet controlled, propulsive thrust generated by the hindquarters into the athletic movement of the horse.

Impulsion (*Engagement and the Desire to Go Forward*)

In the German translation of the Training Scale, the quality of impulsion is called *Schwung,* which is the condition in which the energy created by the hind legs is transmitted through a swinging back and manifested in the horse's elastic, whole-bodied movement. The swinging back has elastic, positive tension, and the energy from the hind legs is transmitted through this swinging body to the bit. In this state we say the horse has developed "throughness" or, in German, *Durchlässigkeit*.

When the horse develops this impulsion or *Schwung*, the rhythm becomes more defined and is called *cadence*. The USDF says that cadence is the "marked accentuation of the rhythm and beat that is a result of a steady and suitable tempo harmonizing with a springy impulsion." This is a good example of how the quality of the basics should improve as the horse develops through the levels. The rhythm improves and becomes cadenced.

Impulsion is first officially required in the dressage tests at First Level where the horse is asked to lengthen the stride in both trot and canter. The horse with impulsion and *Schwung* goes promptly forward from the rider's leg. This is different from the horse going on his own or running.

The energy goes from the hindquarters through the back to the bit *and* it returns to the hind leg. From the USDF definition, you see that it is not only the desire to go forward, but it is also engagement. Once the energy gets to the bit, what happens? The horse doesn't just lean on the bit and plow forward. The half-halts and transitions help him carry himself upright and the energy gets transferred back to a hind foot that is flat on the ground so he can carry weight (engage) with it. So, that energy from the thrusting hind leg gets recycled. Pushing power from the hind legs is balanced by carrying power of those same hind legs. They push and they carry. The rider is in charge of the ratio between pushing power and carrying power.

Straightness *(Improved Alignment and Equal Lateral Suppleness on Both Reins)*

When your horse is straight, he should be able to thrust and carry equally with both hind legs, but horses, like people, favor one side or the other. They are naturally stronger on one side and weaker on the other in the same way that people are right- or left-handed. Secondly, the hips of horses are wider than their shoulders. Left to their own devices, horses typically step outside the center of gravity because it's simply easier for them. This causes the common problem of being "wide behind."

As a result of this normal inclination, trainers are constantly trying to narrow the hind legs and ask the horse to step under his center of gravity in "shoulder-fore." The horse steps under the rider's seat with his inside hind leg without allowing the outside hind leg to go out.

The horse should always be straightened by mobilizing the shoulders to be in front of the hindquarters, which transfers weight to the hind legs. For example, serpentines and figure eights mobilize the horse's shoulders to the right and then to the left, and when your horse is able to bend left and right equally well, he can easily be straightened. Counter-canter is another ideal straightening exercise because it helps the rider control the horse's shoulders and keep them in front of the hindquarters. When the horse is straight, each hind leg is willing and able to carry the same amount of weight in half-halts and collecting exercises.

When you have Impulsion and Straightness (the fourth and fifth elements of the Training Scale)—as well as the first three—you can have the sixth and final one, Collection, on a silver platter. It "just happens." Collection of the first, second, or third degree is the ultimate goal for a dressage horse or for a jumping horse because it provides enough maneuverability, grace, and strength to achieve the task at hand.

USDF DEFINITION:
★ Collection (Balance and Lightness of the Forehand from Increased Engagement)

The horse shows collection when he lowers and engages his hindquarters, shortening and narrowing his base of support, resulting in lightness and mobility of the forehand. He shows shorter but powerful, cadenced steps and strides. The increased elevation must be the result of and relative to the lowering of the hindquarters.

Collection (Balance and Lightness of the Forehand from Increased Engagement)

Ideally, if the horse's training has progressed with careful attention to the basics of the Training Scale, collection is a by-product of the system. The horse moves forward in a clear and steady rhythm. The neck and back are supple and loose. The horse reaches honestly for the bridle as he thrusts from behind. He is developed equally left and right. Collection can't exist without all of those basic principles that are established day after day, year after year.

Collection is first required at Second Level. Whereas collection is a natural by-product of correct training, there are exercises that directly improve the collection.

For example:

• Half-halts directly transfer weight to the hindquarters.

• Rein-back directly does the same, and the rider needs to be careful to retain the engagement when he goes forward out of the rein-back.

• Lateral exercises with bend improve the connection as well as the collection. When you add forward activity such as the medium gaits, before or after the lateral work, it improves the collection by adding power and lift.

• Transitions that skip a gait such as canter-walk-canter or trot-halt-trot improve the collection by increasing the engagement in the downward transition and improving the thrust in the upward transition.

As a result of these collecting exercises, the frame of the horse becomes shorter and more uphill, making the front end freer. Because the horse retains his activity, the shorter stride becomes more elevated. The head and neck come up as a result of the withers coming up. The amount of freedom and lift of the forehand depends on the degree of engagement. When the head and neck come up but the withers stay low, the horse has lost his throughness and the use of his back, and the rider needs to regain that.

The concept of collection at Second Level is exactly the same as the concept of collection at Grand Prix, but it is a matter of degree. When the horse is appropriately collected for his level, the work at that level is easy.

The first degree of collection is that of a four- or five-year-old horse who is able to do Training and First Level.

The second degree of collection is that degree that is introduced at Second Level where the "collected trot" and "collected canter" are required. The horse's back may not be strong enough for him to carry his frame perfectly, but it is the beginning.

USDF DEFINITION:
★ *Throughness (A Shortening of "Throughlettingness," the Literal Translation of the German term Durchlässigkeit)*

An equestrian term that means the supple, elastic, unblocked, connected state of the horse's musculature and a willing mental state that permits an unrestricted flow of energy from back to front and front to back (circle of the aids), which allows the aids/influences to go through all parts of the horse.

Obedience is submission in reference to the accurate performance of the required exercise, in contrast to submission in regard to the basics. The horse may demonstrate resistance or evasion (lack of submission in the basics), yet still be "obedient." For example, if the horse performs a series of flying changes without mistakes and in the correct place but is behind the vertical, tilting his head and swishing his tail, he performs the exercise obediently, but is not submissive in regard to the basics.

The horse in third-degree collection carries at least 55 percent of his weight behind and a minimum of 45 percent in front. As a result, he carries himself in an uphill frame with his withers high, and he is highly maneuverable. The work is easy because the horse has gone through months and years of body-building with suppling and strengthening exercises. He and his rider move as one.

Throughness and Obedience

As a result of your persistent but patient pursuit of the basics of the Training Scale, throughness and obedience develop. These qualities epitomize the harmonious partnership that equestrians strive for!

● The Purposes of Dressage Tests

If you're a dressage rider, it's advisable that you know *why* you're doing the test—even if you're not competing. "The purpose of the test" is what you will be judged on in your general work, whether by a real judge or by yourself, your instructor, and your friends. It's also a checklist that is related to the Training Scale. You will see the elements of the Training Scale in bold throughout the "purposes" through Second Level—at which point Collection, the final element, has been achieved. After Second Level, all the qualities of the Training Scale improve bit by bit.

These dressage tests reflect the collective genius of generations of great horsemen, and they reflect the Training Scale. Paying attention to them pays off!

How Two Minds Meet:
The Mental Dynamics
of Dressage

- **The Purpose of Introductory Level**—To introduce the rider and/or horse to the sport of dressage. To show understanding of riding the horse forward with a steady **tempo** into an elastic **contact** with independent, steady hands, and a correct balanced seat. To show proper geometry of figures in the arena with correct bend (corners and circles).

- **The Purpose of Training Level**—To confirm that the horse demonstrates correct basics, is **supple** and moves freely forward in a clear **rhythm** with a steady tempo, accepting **contact** with the bit.

- **The Purpose of First Level**—To confirm that the horse demonstrates correct basics, and in addition to the requirements of Training Level, has developed the **thrust (impulsion)** to achieve improved balance and throughness, and maintains a more consistent contact with the bit.

- **The Purpose of Second Level**—To confirm that the horse demonstrates correct basics, and having achieved the **thrust** (**impulsion**) required in First Level, now accepts more weight on the hindquarters (**collection**); moves with an uphill tendency, especially in the medium gaits; and is reliably on the bit. A greater degree of **straightness**, bending, **suppleness**, throughness, balance, and self-carriage is required than at First Level.

- **The Purpose of Third Level**—To confirm that the horse demonstrates correct basics, and having begun to develop an uphill balance at Second Level, now demonstrates increased engagement, especially in the extended gaits. Transitions between collected, medium, and extended gaits should be well defined and performed with engagement. The horse should be reliably on the bit and show a greater degree of **straightness**, bending, **suppleness**, **throughness**, balance, and self-carriage than at Second Level.

- **The Purpose of Fourth Level**—To confirm that the horse demonstrates correct basics and has developed sufficient **suppleness, impulsion,** and **throughness** to perform the Fourth Level tests, which have a medium degree of difficulty. The horse remains reliably on the bit, showing a clear uphill balance and lightness as a result of improved **engagement** and **collection**. The movements are performed with greater **straightness**, energy, and cadence than at Third Level.

Acknowledgments

How Two Minds Meet:
The Mental Dynamics
of Dressage

One of my earliest interests outside of horses was educational psychology and the workings of the mind. I noticed, in the early days of dressage in the United States, how a few European trainers—notably Kyra Kyrklund and Conrad Schumacher—stressed the importance of learning psychology and how to utilize it for both horses and riders. For them, riding wasn't just about physics but included how horses and riders absorbed information and how they felt. Sensation played a role in their sport.

Decades ago, on these shores, I remember Kathy Connelly saying that someday, the vast majority of riders would become so skilled physically that winners would be determined by the mind, the heart, and the soul.

Thankfully, there are now many trainers in the United States who demonstrate enormous depth of knowledge that goes way beyond physical technique. They know how horses think, and they constantly help riders to understand life from the horse's point of view. To name a few who are especially talented in this department, I think of Sue Blinks, Charlotte Bredahl, Kathy Connelly, Scott Hassler, Debbie MacDonald, George Williams, and my daughter Jennifer. Leading trainers in the USDF Certified Instructor program—notably Lilo Fore, Sarah Geikie, and Lendon Gray, within my realm of experience—incorporate the mental as well as the physical into their teaching, either because they do it naturally or because they have been educated in psychology. The USDF Certification program embraces the feelings and perceptions of both horse and rider. Many thanks, not only to these trainers, but also to the many others I've failed to mention.

On a far more fundamental level, thanks goes to the non-riders in my family—my husband Alan and our sons, Kevin and Karl—all of whom would often have preferred to be rallying around a hockey arena instead of a dressage arena. They encouraged me and daughter Jennifer to follow our hearts into this crazy love of horses.

And, of course, thanks to the team at Trafalgar Square Books: Caroline Robbins, Rebecca Didier, and Martha Cook. They're the best in the business.

Index

Index

Index

Index

Index

Index